*Praise for*
# PROTECTING THE BRAND

"As the author states in his very first line: 'A brand can be a company's most valuable asset.' Unfortunately, the simple truth of this statement is too often belied by the knowledge of and importance many professional managers attach to effectively managing and supporting the brand. The author provides that manager with a valuable and highly readable treatise on the legal and managerial issues involved in trademarks and brand management.... Timely and well-written, this book is a valuable addition to the literature of trademarks and brand management."

> —Todd Dickinson, Partner, Howrey Simon Arnold & White,
> Former Under Secretary of Commerce for Intellectual Property and
> Director of the United States Patent and Trademark Office

"This book should be required reading for every in-house lawyer—indeed, it should be required reading for anyone who regularly provides legal services to clients with brands to protect. That's because the law of trademarks, service marks, and trade names is far from intuitive, and a well-intentioned but ill-informed lawyer can inadvertently do great damage to his/her client's best interests unless equipped with the concepts in this most readable of primers.... [T]his book is easy to grasp, clear, and concise. It is a pleasure and an honor to recommend it without qualification."

> —Anne H. McNamara, Former Senior Vice President and General
> Counsel, AMR Corp., parent company of American Airlines, Inc.

"As lead attorney for the AAdvantage program, the world's largest customer loyalty program, I counted on Tal Franklin for practical and understandable guidance on protecting and monitoring the use of this and other valuable trademarks around the world. In *Protecting the Brand*, Tal continues in this vein by reducing the arcane legal technicalities of trademark law to succinct and practical rules and tips on how to effectively create, use, maintain, license and enforce your marks. This handy and useful guide is a welcome resource for in-house counsel and other non-specialists charged with protecting what may be a company's most valuable asset."

> —Tobin K. Clark, Senior Vice President,
> General Counsel and Secretary, IMCO Recycling Inc.

"Talcott Franklin is a lawyer and teacher who understands the business person's need for direct information without legalese. In *Protecting the Brand*, Tal again cuts to the chase, providing key information in a concise and easy-to-follow format."

—Holly Stroud, Former Vice President & General Counsel, American Eagle Airlines, Inc.

"Talcott Franklin has written a book that is highly informative, pleasurably readable, and utterly practical; but what is more important, he has incorporated examples and opinions that show how crucial a knowledge of linguistics is for the protection of a brand, all laced together in a step-by-step manual format."

—Donald D. Hook, Ph.D., Professor *emeritus* of Modern Languages and Linguistics, Trinity College, Hartford, Connecticut

"Written in an informal and highly readable style, [*Protecting the Brand*] successfully pierces the veil of what for many lawyers and most laymen has heretofore been a virtually impenetrable mystery. For all who have embraced the commercial world's current branding craze, as well as all who have not yet done so, this book is a must."

—Sydnor Thompson, Jr., Former Judge, North Carolina Court of Appeals

"In writing a 'how to' book for protecting brands, Talcott Franklin offers principles illustrated by hundreds of actual examples of correct and incorrect practices, many involving familiar brands. The result is a fascinating glimpse into a little known aspect of our society whose consequences range from the rise and fall of companies to the addition of new words to our lexicon. This very readable treatment should be of great interest to social scientists concerned with the dynamics of organizations and influences on American culture."

—David R. Schmitt, Professor of Sociology, *Emeritus*, University of Washington

"Franklin's *Protecting the Brand* is a readable yet legally sophisticated introduction to establishing and protecting trademarks; because of its practical focus, it should be required reading for anyone in business today. Humorous examples and familiar product stories make the book especially accessible, while the attention to actual legal cases and principles give Franklin's recommendations a special credibility in today's "how-to" book market. Law and business school students will be particularly interested in this book."

—Dr. David S. Caudill, Professor of Law, Washington and Lee University

# PROTECTING THE BRAND

## TALCOTT J. FRANKLIN, J.D., M.A.

BARRICADE
BOOKS

FORT LEE, NEW JERSEY

Published by Barricade Books Inc.
185 Bridge Plaza North
Suite 308-A
Fort Lee, NJ 07024
www.barricadebooks.com

Library of Congress Cataloging-in-Publication Data

Franklin, Talcott J.
    Protecting the brand / Talcott J. Franklin.
        p. cm.
    ISBN 1-56980-257-2 (hard cover)
    1. Brand name products--Management. 2. Brand name products--
Valuation--Management. 3. Intangible property--Valuation--Management. I.
Title.

HD69.B7F727 2003
658.8'27--dc21

2003048141

Manufactured in the United States of America
First Printing

# CONTENTS

# CONTENTS

# INTRODUCTION

A brand can be a company's most valuable asset. Because the brand is an intangible asset, however, many companies do not understand how to protect it. If the brand were a billion-dollar mansion, the company would outfit it with golden chandeliers, leather chairs, antique tables, and Persian rugs. The company would protect the house with titanium locks, guard dogs, iron fences, and a security system.

Would the company leave those doors unlocked and the security system off? Would it loan the house to biker gangs and football hooligans for unchaperoned beer bashes? Amazingly, numerous sophisticated companies do the equivalent to their brands and then gasp in amazement as the courts find that the company behaved so irresponsibly that the brand is taken from it.

A simple glance through the dictionary confirms this little publicized fact. Words like aspirin, brassiere, cellophane, cube steak, dry ice, escalator, gold card, gramophone, ice beer, kerosene, lanolin, light beer, linoleum, mimeograph, nylon, pilates, raisin bran, shredded wheat, space shuttle, super glue, thermos, trampoline, yo-yo, and zipper now enrich our language because a court found that the owners of these brands did not have the exclusive right to use them—essentially a "death penalty" for brands.

7

# INTRODUCTION

A brand that anyone can use has no value. For a brand to have value, it must become a trademark so that the owner essentially holds a monopoly over a symbol that the public could otherwise use. To retain this monopoly, the owner must follow certain rules of use. Although these rules seem picky and therefore insignificant, following them is essential to retaining a healthy trademark. In fact, mark owners have seen their trademarks sentenced to death for the simple crime of designating a mark with an ® instead of a ™, failing to use the mark as an adjective, or letting someone else use the mark without monitoring their use.

Such a disaster can be difficult to prevent without knowing the rules governing trademark use. This book sets forth these rules in simple, easy-to-read language, along with the rationale for the rules and sample cases that demonstrate how and why the courts apply the rules. It also provides practical tips on how to create and maintain a brand defense strategy.

The first section explains the principles underlying the single most important aspect of brand value: exclusivity. It defines trademarks and other relevant terms, demonstrates why trademarks are both valuable assets and essential to commerce, and explains why courts require such high standards from trademark owners.

The second section covers the trademark-use rules and is divided into two parts. Part A gives the general rules for retaining and managing trademarks. Part B provides the rules for using trademarks in text. This section follows a simple format designed to enhance the understanding of difficult concepts. By presenting the rule, the reason for the rule, a quotation from a court about the rule, and an illustrative case where a court punished a trademark holder for not following the rule, the book moves through progressively deeper levels of analysis. This allows an understanding of *why* each rule exists and therefore makes following it much more likely.

Finally, the third section provides practical tips on how to protect and keep a brand alive.

This book is written with the goal of raising awareness and simplifying a complex subject. Consequently, numerous details, subtleties, nuances, and variations must be omitted. **This book is not a substitute for obtaining competent trademark counsel to manage your brand.**

*Notes on terminology:*

I use the term "product" to refer to both goods and services. This is because, technically, services are covered by service marks, goods are covered by trademarks, and trademarks is also used in the broader sense to cover trademarks, service marks, and trade dress.

I sometimes use the terms brand, trademark, and mark interchangeably. In common use, the dictionary defines brand as "a trademark *or* distinctive name identifying a product or a manufacturer." Thus, keep in mind that a brand is not always a trademark.

Some of these uses may cause the hard-shelled technician to scream. The problem with most books covering this subject on the market today, however, is that the lack of simplification has caused many to remain ignorant rather than wade through the parsing of terms and the exceptions to the exceptions. This book is not for the hard-shelled technician. It is for the class of folks that, to quote one of my mentors, "have to this point lived a full, happy, meaningful life without ever thinking about intellectual property."

# PART I

## The Principles of Brands

**A brand is a symbol that answers the question "Where did this come from?"**

A trademark is a word, name, symbol, phrase, logo, color, sound, smell, or other marking (or combination of any of these) that lets consumers know who provides a particular product. Just like a brand on a steer identifies the ranch to which the steer belongs, a product's trademark (loosely called a brand) answers the question "Where did this come from?"

The government grants a trademark owner what amounts to a monopoly over using a trademark so that the public can readily identify the providers of goods and services. Without such a monopoly, businesses could circulate inferior products under their competitors' marks. This could deceive the public into buying inferior products and tarnish the reputation of the providers of high-quality products.

Distinguishing the *source* of a product, rather than the product itself, is an important concept. For example, "Water" cannot serve as a trademark for $H_2O$ because when the public asks for "water," they want $H_2O$, regardless of who processes, bottles, or sells it. By contrast, when the public asks for "Evian Bottled Water," it wants water from the French Alps aquifer that flows to the French town of Evian-les-Bains and is sold by the Danone Group. The shortcut to asking for this product is the trademark "Evian."

11

When a trademark comes to symbolize the product *itself*, rather than the provider of the product, it ceases to be a trademark, and anyone can use it to describe *his or her own* similar product. This can occur when a brand becomes so successful that consumers refer to the product by the brand name alone.

This is why the Coca-Cola Company gets upset when a waiter brings a "Pepsi" cola to someone who asks for a "Coke." If the public begins to see "Coke" as just another word for "cola" (no matter who makes it), then the Coca-Cola Company could lose the valuable mark "Coke."

Thus, trademark owners, as holders of a monopoly, have a responsibility to ensure that the trademark represents their *provision of* the product instead of the *name of* the product itself. Once a mark ceases to answer the question "Where did this come from?" and starts to answer the question "What is this?" the government will no longer protect the trademark holder's monopoly over using the mark.

For example, "Cellophane" was once the Dupont Cellophane Company's brand name for transparent sheets of regenerated cellulose. Unfortunately, no one called these transparent sheets anything but cellophane, even when attempting to order the product from Dupont's competitors. Consequently, a court found that it would be unfair to allow Dupont to have a monopoly over a word commonly used to describe the product. Dupont lost the trademark, and "cellophane" went into the dictionary as an ordinary word.

## Trademarks, patents, and copyrights are not created equal

Many people confuse trademarks with patents or copyrights. Both patents and copyrights developed in response to the United States Constitution's mandate granting Congress the power to "promote the progress of science and useful arts, by securing for limited times to authors and inventors the exclusive right to their respective writings and discoveries." Trademarks did not develop from the Constitution, but from judicial decisions, and later from legislation called the Lanham Act, in response to the need to distinguish one manufacturer's product from another's.

A patent protects inventions and discoveries, such as a better mousetrap, an improved golf club head design, or a system for recycling waste material. The patent statute allows patents for anyone who "invents or discovers any new and useful process, machine, manufacture, or composition of matter, or any new and useful improvement thereof."

A patent is basically a bargain with the government in which the inventor tells the public how the invention is made, and in exchange, the government gives the inventor a monopoly for a limited period of time on making, using, or selling the invention. This allows an inventor the opportunity to profit from the invention while still letting the public know how it is made. The inventor need not worry during that limited period of protection that the invention will be stolen and marketed by others.

A patent does not take effect until it is applied for and granted by the United States Patent and Trademark Office. The patent generally lasts for twenty years from the date on which the patent application was filed, although different time periods may apply in special cases.

Copyrights protect artistic expressions such as drawings, books, poems, choreography, songs, architecture, and motion pictures. A copyright protects the expression itself, not the ideas expressed. These concepts can be difficult to separate, but a clear line can be drawn between language and information. For example, others can report the general information I convey in this book without violating my copyright. Copying my words, pictures, or format, however, may violate my copyright.

A copyright automatically attaches to any written work upon creation. For works created on or after January 1, 1978, copyright protection generally lasts for the author's lifetime plus seventy years after the author's death. Different time periods apply to coauthors (the authors' lifetimes plus seventy years after the last surviving author's death) and to works for hire and anonymous or pseudonymous works (the shorter of ninety-five years from publication or 120 years from creation). Copyright owners have the option of registering their copyright with the United States Copyright Office, but registration is not necessary for copyright protection. Registration is necessary, however, to bringing an infringement action in court based on a work originated in the United States.

As stated in the Constitution, patent and copyright protection eventually expires so that the public can use the holder's work and thus promote scientific and artistic progress. By contrast, trademark rights can last in perpetuity, assuming the trademark owner properly uses the trademark.

The expiration of patents and copyrights as opposed to the perpetual nature of trademarks underscores the fundamental purposes of these protections. Patents and copyrights exist to encourage people to disclose their inventions and art so that the public can ultimately appropriate and benefit from the creator's work. When a patent or copyright expires, any member of the public can use the invention or artistic work.

By contrast, trademarks exist so that the public can discern who provides certain products or services. If a trademark falls into the public domain—so that it is no longer associated with a certain provider of goods and services—then the trademark has little value. A trademark that remains exclusive, however, grows in value because the public increasingly associates it with a single company. This exclusivity is at the heart of what marketing experts call "brand identity" —the consumer's immediate reaction to viewing the company trademark. A consumer who sees the brand must know that it is exclusive to the company. Otherwise, a consumer cannot associate the brand with a consistent set of expectations and experiences.

### A brand is a shortcut

Trademarks serve as a shortcut: an easy way for consumers to associate a service or product with quality, value, prestige, and other attributes. For example, seeing the Golden Arches may bring to mind hamburgers (the product), NBA basketball (sponsorship), family fun (advertisement), Ronald McDonald house (charity), instant winners (promotion), and convenience (service).

Thus, a trademark can symbolize all the attributes of a particular business. If a mark holder can achieve this association, then the mark has incredible value. For example, when consumers drive on a busy street, it is hoped that they are watching for traffic and trying to find their way. They do not have the time or the ability to read a detailed description of every restaurant on the street. However, a mere glimpse of the Golden Arches has the same effect as a sign reading:

For Sale: Quick, tasty, and inexpensive hamburgers loved by professional basketball stars, served in a clean, family-friendly, and courteous environment. A portion of the purchase price goes to charity, and you may win valuable prizes. Inquire at speakerphone or within.

In fact, the brand has a greater effect on a consumer than any detailed sign ever will because the brand also conveys the consumer's personal experiences as well as the image the advertiser wants to sell.

### Brands sum up a consumer's experiences

Say you visit a restaurant called "Joe Bob's Barbeque." It has a red-and-white sign shaped like a pig, a flat red roof with a brick exterior, and clean, pleasantly spaced tables with red-and-white-checkered tablecloths. You experience friendly, efficient service, have the best barbeque you have ever eaten, and are pleasantly surprised to receive a bill that is half of what you expected to pay.

A month later, you visit a "Joe Bob's Barbeque" in another town. It looks the same, and you have the same great experience. You even meet the owner, a friendly, lively man named Joe Bob Smith, who tells you "we're expanding all over the state, so I hope you get a chance to visit our other locations."

One month later, you see a red-and-white sign shaped like a pig for "Joe Bob's BBQ." You eagerly stop to eat there, with your mouth watering in anticipation. It has the same red roof and checkered tablecloths, but the tables are crowded together and dirty, the staff is unfriendly and lazy, the food tastes terrible, and the bill is outrageously high. You leave disgusted, thinking Joe Bob expanded too fast or, worse yet, got greedy and jacked up the prices while lowering the restaurant quality.

You decide to never go back to "Joe Bob's Barbeque." Unfortunately, Joe Bob Smith did not own the restaurant you last visited. Bill Johnson, an ex-con turned trademark infringer owned "Joe Bob's BBQ." But by the time the real Joe Bob put Bill out of business, you—and hundreds of others—have decided never to visit another Joe Bob's based on one rotten experience with an infringed trademark.

Joe Bob spent thousands of dollars each year on advertising, building good will, and improving his product and service so that his customers would view his chain in a positive light, and, it was hoped, have those good experiences influence their buying decisions. His trademark—the red-and-white sign shaped like a pig that said "Joe Bob's Barbeque"—represented the culmination of those experiences in a simple, easy-to-recognize format. Unfortunately, Bill Johnson capitalized on Joe Bob's trademark to turn a fast buck—and ruined Joe Bob's good name in the process.

This story illustrates the importance of a trademark: It symbolizes the sum of all experiences a consumer has with a product. If the trademark is exclusive to its owner, and the owner provides consistently superior products, then the trademark will have incredible value. If, by contrast, the trademark becomes associated with inferior products, then the trademark may have negative value.

## Brands are worth their weight in gold

As the previous discussion demonstrates, an exclusive trademark associated with consistently superior products will have incredible value. But how much value? This will depend on a variety of factors, some of which are beyond the trademark holder's control, such as the state of the economy. A well-protected trademark, however, can be a company's most valuable asset.

For example, according to the 2002 version of an annual survey conducted by Interbrand Corporation published in the August 5,

2002, issue of *BusinessWeek* magazine, the top ten brands had a value ranging from $68.64 billion ("Coca-Cola") to $21.01 billion ("Mercedes").

Brand value stems more from earning power than prestige. For example, in the 2001 version of the survey (published in the August 6, 2001, issue of *BusinessWeek* magazine), the "Toyota" brand ranked fourteenth ($18.58 billion), while the "BMW" brand ranked twenty-second ($13.86 billion). Yet who makes the more prestigious automobile? Toyota basically admits that it cannot compete in BMW's market by carrying its own luxury brand—"Lexus." Toyota has a more valuable brand than BMW because, given the competition, Toyota's core values—reliability and economy—carry more value in the overall marketplace than BMW's core values—meticulous engineering and luxury.

The "Mercedes" brand, ranked twelfth, topped both companies' brand values in 2001 at $21.73 billion due to its domination of the luxury sedan market, but even the "Mercedes" brand lagged behind the good old "Ford" brand, ranked eighth in 2001 at $30.09 billion. After a bitter divorce from longtime business partner Firestone and questions about the stability of its SUVs, the "Ford" brand lost nearly $10 billion in value, falling to number eleven on the 2002 list at $20.40 billion. By essentially holding steady, the "Mercedes" brand moved up to number ten. Meanwhile, a tough economy helped the "Toyota" brand rise to number twelve on the 2002 list, at $19.45 billion.

The value of these brands underscores their need for diligent protection. For example, Interbrand values the "McDonald's" brand (ranked eighth) at $26.38 billion. According to McDonald's 2000 Annual Report, McDonald's tangible assets are valued at $21.863 billion. Thus, one could make a case that McDonald's would be in better fiscal shape if a financial disaster wiped out all its tangible assets than if a lawsuit wiped out its trademark.

Moving far down the Interbrand survey rankings, the "FedEx" brand ranked eighty-sixth in 2001, with a value of $1.86 billion. According to FedEx Corporation's 2001 Annual Report, FedEx's capital expenditures for 2001 were roughly $1.89 billion. Thus, if FedEx lost its brand, the financial toll could equate to losing a year's worth of capital expenditures—a brutal blow to any company.

FedEx devotes significant resources to protecting the planes, facilities, and technology purchased with its capital expenditures. Security guards, locks, fences, and video surveillance undoubtedly protect these investments from thieves while contracts reviewed by lawyers and management protect the assets from repossession.

Should FedEx—or any other corporation for that matter—spend an equivalent amount of time, money, and energy protecting the brand? As this book will demonstrate, one badly managed contract can result in a company losing its brand, which could cause far more damage than losing any single physical asset.

## Trademark friends and family

**Trademark**
Any word, name, phrase, logo, slogan, symbol, source indicator, or any combination of these adopted to distinguish *goods* from those of others. For example, "Budweiser" for beer made by Anheuser-Busch Incorporated. Also used generically to encompass trademarks, service marks, and trade dress.

**Service mark**
Any word, name, phrase, logo, slogan, symbol, source indicator, or any combination of these adopted to distinguish *services* from those of others. For example, "Greyhound" for transportation services provided by Greyhound Lines, Incorporated.

® is attached to marks that are registered with the appropriate governmental agency (such as the United States Patent and Trademark Office).

TM is attached to trademarks about which no claim of registration is being made.

SM is attached to service marks about which no claim of registration is being made.

Other intellectual property symbols that **do not** indicate trademarks include the following:

- © means an author is claiming copyright protection for a work. A work containing a trademark can be copyrighted, but copyright protection is not generally sought for the trademark itself. The copyright notice should have three elements: (1) the circle "C"; (2) the copyright owner's name; and (3) the year of first publication. For example:

  © 2003 Talcott J. Franklin

- ℗ means an author is claiming copyright protection for a phonorecord of a sound recording. The phonorecord copyright notice should have three elements: (1) the circle "P"; (2) the copyright owner's name; and (3) the year of first publication. For example:

  ℗ 2003 Talcott J. Franklin

The copyright office has published guidelines for properly affixing the copyright notice to artistic works in the Code of Federal Regulations. 37 C.F.R. § 201.20.

- "Patent Pending" or "Patent Applied For" means that an inventor, manufacturer, or seller of an article has filed a patent application with the United States Patent and Trademark Office. These notices have no legal effect except to give notice that a patent application has been filed.

- "Patent No. _____" means that the invention is patented. The number is assigned by the United States Patent and Trademark Office so others can look up and identify the corresponding patent. Failure to mark the invention may prevent the patent owner from recovering damages from an infringer unless the infringer was notified of the patent and continued to infringe after notification.

**Trade dress**
The overall graphics and shape of a product or its packaging adopted

to distinguish goods or services from those of others. Courts have ruled that the following constitute a trade dress: Philip Morris' Marlboro Man (*Philip Morris Inc. v. Star Tobacco Corp.*, 879 F. Supp. 379, 383 (S.D.N.Y. 1995)), Pepperidge Farm's goldfish-shaped crackers (*Nabisco, Inc. v. PF Brands, Inc.*, 191 F.3d 208, 217 (2d Cir. 1999)), Ferrari's automotive body design (*Esercizio v. Roberts*, 944 F.2d 1235, 1240 (6th Cir. 1991)), Pebble Beach's golf hole with a lighthouse (*Pebble Beach Co. v. Tour 18 I Ltd.*, 155 F.3d 526, 541 (5th Cir. 1998)), and even the distinctive performing style of a rock band (*Cesare v. Work*, 520 N.E.2d 586, 593 (Ohio App. 1987)).

**Trade name**
The name of a business. It is not a trademark. Some businesses will use a portion of their trade name as a trademark, however.

Examples:

| | |
|---|---|
| The Coca-Cola Company | "Coca-Cola" |
| The Ford Motor Company | "Ford" |
| Microsoft Corporation | "Microsoft" |
| eBay Incorporated | "eBay" |
| Amazon.com Incorporated | "Amazon.Com" |
| Texaco Incorporated | "Texaco" |
| Starbucks Coffee Company | "Starbucks" |
| McDonald's Corporation | "McDonald's" |

## Registration is not a silver bullet

Many trademark owners believe they can hold up their trademark registration like a cross to ward off all evils that might befall their trademark. This is simply false. Trademark registration creates certain advantages in the event of a lawsuit involving the trademark, but it does not protect the trademark owner against its own abuse of the mark. The United States Patent and Trademark Office Web site lists only the following advantages to registration:

- constructive notice to the public of the registrant's claim of ownership of the mark;

- a legal presumption of the registrant's ownership of the mark and the registrant's exclusive right to use the mark nationwide on or in connection with the goods and/or services listed in the registration;

- the ability to bring an action concerning the mark in federal court;

- the use of the U.S. registration as a basis to obtain registration in foreign countries; and

- the ability to file the U.S. registration with the U.S. Customs Service to prevent importation of infringing foreign goods.

As one federal appeals court commented: "Mere registration under the Federal Act does not create a trade-mark and confers no new rights to the mark claimed, nor, indeed, any greater rights than already existed at common law without registration. Registration is a method of recording for the protection of dealers, the public, and owners of trade-marks. It is notice of the claims of the owner affecting his right to the mark. But the right to such a trade-mark must have accrued from actual use, because such right is not created by registration of the mark." *Walgreen Drug Stores v. Obear-Nester Glass Co.*, 113 F.2d 956, 960 (8th Cir. 1940).

Thus, trademark registration is not an essential element of trademark protection. It does, however, tell the public that the trademark owner is serious about the trademark and has taken action to protect it.

Trademark owners apply for registration by submitting to the USPTO a written application form, a drawing of the mark, a filing fee, and, if the application is based on prior use of the mark in commerce, three actual examples of the mark as it is used in each class of goods or services for which it is being registered. Actual examples of use of the mark on goods include a tag or label, a container, or a photograph of the goods bearing the mark. Actual examples of use for services include a sign, a brochure, or an advertisement.

The USPTO registers marks in different classes to avoid granting a trademark owner exclusive rights to a mark in all areas of commerce. For example, a maker of radios could register the mark "Blast Box" in class 9 (which includes "apparatus for recording, transmission or reproduction of sound or images"). A toy maker might simultaneously attempt to use the mark "Blast Box" to designate a toy laser in class 28 (which includes games and playthings). The USPTO might allow both registrations to proceed if the marks are dissimilar in appearance and the products sufficiently unrelated so that no one could confuse "Blast Box" radios with "Blast Box" toy lasers.

After the trademark owner files the application, an examining attorney employed by the USPTO will determine if the mark is confusingly similar to another mark. The examining attorney might also refuse registration if the mark merely describes the product or service (e.g., "AM/FM" for radios, "Car" for automobiles, or "Gun" for firearms), is deceptive (e.g., "American Made" for products made in Japan), is primarily a surname, or is ornamental.

If the examining attorney approves the mark, the USPTO publishes it in the USPTO's weekly publication, the *Official Gazette*. If no one files a convincing opposition to the mark, then the USPTO will register the mark and issue a registration certificate for the mark. At this point, the trademark owner may place an ® next to the mark to show that it is registered.

The main disadvantage of trademark registration is the expense associated with filing and maintaining the trademark registration. The main advantage of trademark registration is that until it is disproved, courts will assume that the registrant owns the mark and has the exclusive right to use it nationwide in the manner listed in the registration certificate.

## Hey! That's my brand!

Generally speaking, someone cannot use a mark resembling another party's trademark for commercial gain if the use (1) could lead the public to believe that the trademark owner is somehow affiliated with the user; (2) diminishes the mark's value by associating it with products other than those provided by the trademark owner; or (3) damages the mark's value by associating it with undesirable products.

Some examples of cases where trademark owners successfully prevented others from using similar trademarks include the Dallas Cowboys Cheerleaders preventing the showing and distribution of the film *Debbie Does Dallas*, which the court described as "a gross and revolting sex film whose plot, to the extent that there is one, involves a cheerleader . . . who has been selected to become a 'Texas Cowgirl'" (*Dallas Cowboys Cheerleaders v. Pussycat Cinema, Ltd.*, 604 F.2d 200 (2d Cir. 1979)); Anheuser-Busch preventing an insecticide maker from using the slogan "Where there's life, there's bugs," which traded off Anheuser-Busch's slogan "Where there's life, there's Bud" (*Chemical Corp. of America v. Anheuser-Busch, Inc.*, 306 F.2d 433 (5th Cir. 1962), *cert. denied*, 372 U.S. 965 (1963)); the Coca-Cola Company preventing further distribution of posters with "Enjoy Cocaine" scripted to look like the "Enjoy Coca-Cola" mark (*Coca-Cola Co. v. Gemini Rising, Inc.*, 346 F. Supp. 1183 (E.D.N.Y. 1972)); the maker of "Cabbage Patch Kids" dolls preventing further distribution of "Garbage Pail Kids" stickers and products (*Original Appalachian Artworks, Inc. v. Topps Chewing Gum*, 642 F. Supp. 1031 (N.D. Ga. 1986)); Gucci preventing further distribution of a diaper bag bearing green, red, and green stripes and labeled "Gucchi Goo" (*Gucci Shops, Inc. v. R.H. Macy & Co.*, 446 F. Supp. 838 (S.D.N.Y. 1977)); and General Electric preventing further distribution of t-shirts and underpants containing the monograph "Genital Electric" (*General Electric Co. v. Alumpa Coal Co.*, 205 U.S.P.Q. [BNA] 1036 (D. Mass. 1979)).

Not every unauthorized use of a mark constitutes trademark infringement, however. For example, authors of scholarly works, parodies, or criticisms can generally use the trademarks of others if the use is noncommercial. Such uses should make it clear—by words or context—that the trademark use does not constitute an endorsement by the trademark owner. Thus, Bally Fitness could not prevent a disgruntled consumer from using the "Bally" marks on a Web site titled "Bally Sucks." In fact, the court noted that "An individual who wishes to engage in consumer commentary must have the full range of marks that the trademark owner has to identify the trademark owner as the object of the criticism." *Bally Total Fitness Holding Corp. v. Faber*, 29 F. Supp.2d 1161, 1164 n.4 (C.D. Cal. 1998).

Moreover, the First Amendment may protect even the most objectionable trademark uses. For example, L.L. Bean could not stop *High Society* magazine from publishing a pornographic parody catalogue of *"L.L. Beam"* products without proving that consumers believed that L.L. Bean authorized the parody, even though the magazine admittedly designed the parody to resemble the L.L. Bean catalogue. The court concluded that "Trademark parodies, even when offensive, do convey a message. The message may be simply that business and product images need not always be taken too seriously; a trademark parody reminds us that we are free to laugh at the images and associations linked with the mark. The message also may be a simple form of entertainment conveyed by juxtaposing the irreverent representation of the trademark with the idealized image created by the mark's owner. . . . Denying parodists the opportunity to poke fun at symbols and names which have become woven into the fabric of our daily life, would constitute a serious curtailment of a protected form of expression." *L.L. Bean, Inc. v. Drake Publishers, Inc.*, 811 F.2d 26 (1st Cir. 1987).

## Trademark cases seek the death penalty

If a dispute develops between two parties over the use of a mark, the parties at times will go to court to resolve it. Plaintiffs filing trademark cases generally seek to show that they have the exclusive right to use the mark at issue. The key question is whether the defendant's mark is confusingly similar to the plaintiff's mark so that the defendant's use of the mark has the potential to take away customers who want to deal with the plaintiff. If the answer is "yes," then the defendant generally can no longer use the mark. Thus, if the plaintiff wins, then the defendant's mark essentially receives the death penalty.

The plaintiff's mark can also be at risk, however. Many times, the defendant will claim that the plaintiff does not have a mark at all. The defendant will most often attempt to prove this by showing that 1) the plaintiff's so-called "mark" is actually an ordinary word that anyone can use; or 2) the plaintiff had a mark and quit using it.

When courts analyze whether the plaintiff's mark is an ordinary word (called a "generic" term), they first ask whether most people associate the plaintiff's mark with the plaintiff's products, or whether they associate the plaintiff's mark with the name of the product itself. For example, if most people go to the store and ask for "Kleenex" when all they want is facial tissue, regardless of who makes it, then the mark is generic. A generic term answers the question "What are you?" and does not answer the question "Where did you come from?"

This is a harsh result for the advertiser who spent millions—if not billions—of dollars to "make the mark a household name." Thus, courts often ask whether the plaintiff itself treated the mark as a trademark or a generic term. If the court discovers advertisements, correspondence, or even internal communications where the plaintiff breaks the trademark use rules, then the court will often have little regret in taking the mark away. If the court discovers that the plaintiff went to great lengths to protect the mark, then the court will often be inclined to show leniency on the plaintiff.

When courts analyze whether the plaintiff quit using the mark, they generally ask whether 1) the plaintiff actually used the mark; 2) the plaintiff gave the mark away to someone else; or 3) the plaintiff failed to prevent others from using the mark. If the court finds that the plaintiff did any one of these, then the court can find that the plaintiff abandoned the mark and the defendant can continue using it.

To avoid a finding that the trademark owner no longer has an exclusive right to use the mark, it is important that a trademark holder obey the rules outlined below. Some famous examples of marks that have been lost for failure to obey these rules include aspirin, brassiere, cellophane, cube steak, dry ice, escalator, gold card, gramophone, ice beer, kerosene, lanolin, light beer, linoleum, mimeograph, nylon, pilates, raisin bran, shredded wheat, space shuttle, super glue, thermos, trampoline, yo-yo, and zipper. Thus, a trademark case is essentially a death penalty case because very often the loser's mark dies.

# PART II
## *Brand Use Rules*

A s this section will demonstrate, courts have put to death a significant number of trademarks because the trademark owner failed
to follow the trademark use rules. While courts have, on occa-
sion, punished a trademark owner for a single failure to follow one of
these rules, generally speaking, courts will only invoke the "death
penalty" against an owner's mark if the owner consistently ignores a
rule. Thus, a past failure to follow these rules will not necessarily
result in a lost trademark. Continued disregard of these rules, however, may put the mark in significant peril.

### General Rules of Use

**1. Use it or lose it**

**Rule**: A trademark can be canceled for nonuse.

**Rationale:** Because trademarks are a monopoly over a certain word,
phrase, or symbol, courts will not allow someone to hoard trademarks and deprive the public of an otherwise useful term.

**What the courts say:** "[T]he right to a particular mark grows out of
its use, not its mere adoption . . . it is not the subject of property
except in connection with an existing business." *United Drug Co. v.
Theodore Rectanus Co.*, 248 U.S. 90, 97 (1918).

"[T]rademark rights are not created by sporadic, casual, and nominal shipments of goods bearing a mark. There must be a trade in the goods sold under the mark or at least an active and public attempt to establish such a trade. Absent these elements, no trademark can be created or exist." *La Societe Anonyme des Parfums le Galion v. Patou, Inc.*, 495 F.2d 1265, 1274 (2d. Cir. 1974).

**Illustrative Case:** *Stern Electronics, Inc. v. Kaufman*, 523 F. Supp. 635 (E.D.N.Y. 1981)

**The facts:** In late 1980, a Japanese corporation created a video game called "Scramble," which induced players to intercept enemy jets and blast them out of the sky. In 1981, the Japanese corporation granted Stern Electronics an exclusive sublicense to sell "Scramble," which was fast becoming one of the world's most popular video games.

Prior to Stern receiving its exclusive sublicense, Omni, a competing company, began selling its "Space Guerilla," "Space Carrier," and "Rally-X" video games with headboards bearing the name "Scramble." Less than a month after Stern began selling the Japanese "Scramble" game under the name "Scramble," Omni began selling a similar game called "Scramble 2."

**The dispute:** Stern sued Omni and several other defendants for trademark infringement on the name "Scramble," as well as for copyright violations due to the substantial similarity between Omni's "Scramble 2" video game and Stern's original "Scramble" video game.

**The ruling:** The court granted Stern's request to stop Omni from using the game and the "Scramble 2" mark prior to a full trial. After finding in favor of Stern on the copyright claim, the court turned its attention to whether Omni had established a trademark right in "Scramble" prior to Stern. The court found that despite Omni's earlier use of the "Scramble" mark, Stern owned the trademark:

This court does not find credible the testimony that

defendants decided to use the name "Scramble" before they knew that others had plans to market the new game under the same name. Defendants introduced the name "Scramble" by printing it on headboards attached to video games bearing different names. This practice is likely to confuse customers who can fairly expect that the name on the headboard will match the name of the game. . . . The most likely explanation for this extraordinary marketing decision is that defendants contrived this usage of the mark solely for trademark maintenance purposes in anticipation of plaintiff's introduction of the "Scramble" video game into the market.

The court found Omni's position unsupported by law or credible testimony:

[I]t would be a truly remarkable coincidence if defendants independently thought of the name "Scramble" and then, only a few months later, produced a video game virtually identical to one bearing the same name. It is more likely that defendants sought to appropriate the trademark with the expectation that they would later imitate the audiovisual display. In sum, while the court recognizes that defendants first used the mark "Scramble," it finds that defendants' use of the mark was not bona fide.

Thus, Omni could no longer sell the "Scramble 2" video game or use the "Scramble" and "Scramble 2" marks until the court could more completely determine the issue at trial.

## 2. Don't contribute the mark to the English language

**Rule:** Keep the mark out of the dictionary and the public domain. A mark that becomes the common means of referring to a product, rather than a source of the product, can no longer function as a trademark.

**Rationale:** Courts will not give a trademark owner a monopoly over a word that the public commonly uses to refer to a product. Otherwise, no competitor could market the product without infringing the trademark.

**What the courts say:** "No doubt, the [. . .] doctrine [that takes trademark status away from a mark that has become the common way of referring to the product] can be a harsh one for it places a penalty on the manufacturer who has made skillful use of advertising and has popularized his product. However, King-Seeley has enjoyed a commercial monopoly of the word 'thermos' for over fifty years. During that period, despite its efforts to protect the trademark, the public has virtually expropriated it as its own. The word having become part of the public domain, it would be unfair to unduly restrict the right of a competitor of King-Seeley to use the word." *King-Seeley Thermos Co. v. Aladdin Industries, Inc.*, 321 F.2d 577 (2d Cir. 1963).

**Illustrative case:** *Illinois High School Association v. GTE Vantage*, 99 F.3d 244 (7th Cir. 1996)

**The facts:** Since the 1940s, the Illinois High School Association (IHSA) used the "March Madness" mark to refer to its high school basketball tournament. In 1982, broadcaster Brent Musburger used the phrase to describe the NCAA Final Four Championship basketball games. Musburger's description caught on, and the media and the public began using "March Madness" to designate the NCAA Final Four. In 1993, the NCAA began licensing "March Madness" to producers of goods and services related to the Final Four tournament. In 1996, licensee GTE Vantage began producing a video game called NCAA Championship Basketball, which contained the "March Madness" designation on the box.

**The dispute:** IHSA sued GTE Vantage for trademark infringement to stop GTE Vantage's use of the "March Madness" trademark.

**The ruling:** The court found that IHSA's trademark rights did not extend to the NCAA tournament or merchandise associated with the NCAA tournament. In rejecting IHSA's suit, the court noted that IHSA had the responsibility to prevent the media from damaging its mark:

> It is true that IHSA could not have sued Musburger or CBS for referring to "March Madness" in a news program (including a program of sports news), or even in advertising if the term were used merely for identification. But it could have sued them for using its trademark to promote CBS's broadcast of the NCAA championship. And it could have supplicated them not to spoil its trademark by using it to name something else. A serious trademark holder is assiduous in endeavoring to convince dictionary editors, magazine and newspaper editors, journalists and columnists, judges, and other lexicographically influential persons to avoid using his trademark to denote anything other than the trademarked good or service. These efforts sometimes succeed. IHSA was not assiduous.

The court acknowledged, however, that not even an "assiduous" trademark owner can always prevent its mark from becoming generic:

> When a trademark becomes generic, such as "aspirin" or "thermos," and so loses trademark protection, because the public, perhaps egged on by the omnipresent media, decides to use the trademark to designate not the particular manufacturer's brand but the entire product comprising all the competing brands, the trademark is dead no matter how vigorously the holder has tried to prevent this usage.

Thus, the court refused to allow IHSA to hold a monopoly over the phrase "March Madness" when so many people associated it with the NCAA tournament:

> A trademark owner is not allowed to withdraw from the

public domain a name that the public is using to denote someone else's good or service, leaving that someone and his customers speechless.

### 3. Don't give the mark a split personality

**Rule:** Do not give the mark a definition. Use the mark as a trademark alone, not as the name of the product.

**Rationale:** Marks should identify the source of a product, not the product itself. By giving the mark a definition (other than as a trademark of the company), the mark owner increases the likelihood that the mark will come to identify the product itself rather than the product's source.

**What the courts say:** "The course of conduct of the complainant and its predecessors, and especially the complainant's advertising campaign, tended to make cellophane a generic term descriptive of the product rather than of its origin. . . . The fact that [DuPont] had registered 'Cellophane' as a trade-mark would give it no right to monopolize a term useful to designate a commercial article." *DuPont Cellophane Co., Inc. v. Waxed Products. Co., Inc.,* 85 F.2d 75, 80 (2d Cir. 1936).

**Illustrative case:** *Donald F. Duncan, Inc. v. Royal Tops Manufacturing Co.,* 343 F.2d 655 (7th Cir. 1965)

**The facts:** Duncan began manufacturing return tops under the trademark "Yo-Yo" in 1929 and registered the trademark "Genuine Duncan Yo-Yo" in 1932. In 1955, Duncan started a widespread campaign to name the toy a "return top." Shortly thereafter, Duncan sued several competitors to prevent them from using the "Yo-Yo" trademark.

**The dispute:** Duncan insisted that its founder had invented the term "Yo-Yo" and that when the public saw "Yo-Yo", they thought of a return top manufactured by Duncan. Duncan's competitors argued that the term originated in the Philippines long before Duncan claimed to have coined it, and in any event, the public thought the term "Yo-Yo" was the name of the toy, not an indication of a toy that Duncan manufactured.

**The ruling:** The court found that Duncan had so abused the term "Yo-Yo" that even if Duncan had invented it, it had passed into the public domain. The court based its finding on Duncan's repeated use of the term as though it was the toy's name:

> There is much documentary proof, the authenticity of which is not in dispute, that plaintiff for more than twenty years employed the term "Yo-Yo" in its descriptive and generic sense. Its most publicized slogan used in trade magazines, on the radio, television and otherwise, was "If It Isn't a Duncan, It Isn't a Yo-Yo." "Yo-Yo" as thus used was generic and descriptive of plaintiff's toy. A similar use of "Yo-Yo" in its generic sense in communicating with large numbers of the consumer public was the recording of a song exhorting children to "Spin a Yo-Yo." This recording was plaintiff's theme song, used by plaintiff on a television program which was carried weekly.

The court specifically pointed out that Duncan actually created a definition for the term "Yo-Yo", as though it were the name of the toy rather than a mark for the toy:

> In plaintiff's promotional material a "Yo-Yo" was described as follows: "In case you do not know what a yo-yo is, it's that gaily colored little spool on a string, that in the hands of almost any youngster becomes a thing alive and performs hundreds of fascinating tricks. According to little Joe Radovan, present holder of World's Champion title, yo-yo had its origin in the Philippine Islands over 300 years ago and was used at that time as a weapon."

Although the lower court found that many products are referred to by their trademarks alone and that Duncan should not suffer any consequences for doing the same, the appeals court overruled that position and expressed no sympathy for Duncan's failure to follow the trademark rules:

> We do not agree that plaintiff should be excused from using "Yo-Yo" as the descriptive name for its product, thereby educating the public to treat it as such, because others might use their trademarks in the same manner. Plaintiff, which has enjoyed a monopoly on its trademarks for more than twenty-five years, in our judgment should not be saved from a situation for which it in major part is responsible.

4. **Put it in writing**

**Rule:** Don't grant others permission to use the mark without a written contract. Trademarks can be abandoned. A written contract can make it clear that the other party is using the mark for a limited purpose and has no rights to the mark except as conferred by the trademark owner.

**Rationale:** Trademarks indicate a product's source. If the trademark owner allows those marks to be associated with *any* product, then the mark ceases to act as a source indicator and thus loses its purpose. While a written contract is not the final word, it is evidence that the trademark owner took steps to control the use of the mark, and it will serve as proof of the parties' intentions. Also, a contract can ensure that the mark's good will benefits the trademark holder.

**What the courts say:** "Courts have long imposed upon trademark licensors a duty to oversee the quality of licensees' products. The rationale for this requirement is that marks are treated by purchasers as an indication that the trademark owner is associated with the product. Customers rely upon the owner's reputation when they select the trademarked goods. If a trademark owner allows licensees to depart from its quality standards, the public

ment failed to provide Stanfield any meaningful control over the marks:

> We first review the agreement between the parties for evidence of control. The 1975 agreement did not give plaintiff an express contractual right to inspect or supervise OII's [Osborne's] operations in any way. OII had the right to use the "Stanfield" marks on any of the products it manufactured, including products not developed by plaintiff. Moreover, OII had the "sole discretion" to design the mark. The agreement, then, did not contemplate that plaintiff would have any control of OII's use of the "Stanfield" marks.

While the absence of a control provision did not doom Stanfield's mark (in contrast to the *Robinson* case described in the previous chapter), in examining the course of dealing, the court found that Stanfield did not in fact exercise control over Osborne's use of the mark:

> The absence of an express contractual right of control does not necessarily result in abandonment of a mark, as long as the licensor in fact exercised sufficient control over its licensee. In the instant case, it is undisputed that plaintiff had no contact whatsoever with OII after his employment terminated. Plaintiff contends that he exercised control over OII's use of the "Stanfield" marks by examining one swine heating pad produced by OII, by looking at several pet pads, and by occasionally reviewing OII's promotional materials and advertising. He also contends that his lack of knowledge of any quality control problems is evidence of his control. None of this, however, is evidence that plaintiff actually exercised control over OII.

Stanfield then argued that he felt he could trust Osborne, based on their previous relationship, to exercise adequate care of the marks. The court disagreed, finding that Stanfield could not rely on its business relationship with Osborne to retain control of the mark because no special relationship existed:

> Plaintiff next maintains that he relied on OII for quality control and argues that his reliance on the licensee's quality control is sufficient for him to avoid a finding of a naked license. We disagree.
>
> In cases in which courts have found that a licensor justifiably relied on a licensee for quality control, some special relationship existed between the parties. In *Taco Cabana*, the court examined a cross-license between two brothers who had run a chain of restaurants together for a number of years. When the brothers decided to divide the business, they agreed that both would continue to use the same trade dress in their respective restaurants. Because the parties had maintained a close, long-term working relationship, the court held that they could justifiably rely on each other to maintain quality. In *Transgo*, the licensor itself manufactured at least ninety percent of the goods sold by its licensee, utilizing its own procedures to maintain quality. And in *Land O'Lakes*, the court found that the licensor reasonably relied on the licensee to maintain quality because the parties had maintained a successful association with no consumer complaints for over forty years.

Finally, the court concluded that Stanfield's issuance of a "naked license" resulted in Stanfield abandoning all rights in the marks:

> The terms of the parties' agreement, and their subsequent actions, compel us to hold that the 1975 agreement between plaintiff and OII was a naked license, by which plaintiff abandoned all his rights in the "Stanfield" marks.

## 6. Keep their grubby hands off the mark

**Rule:** Prevent others from infringing on the mark. A trademark owner must take steps to control the unlicensed use of its mark.

**Rationale:** A trademark owner is in the best position to prevent the public confusion that arises when another entity offers products under the mark. Allowing widespread infringement reduces the public's understanding that products bearing the mark are provided by the trademark owner and can weaken the mark or even constitute abandonment of the mark.

**What the courts say:** "Without question, distinctiveness can be lost by failing to take action against infringers. If there are numerous products in the marketplace bearing the alleged mark, purchasers may learn to ignore the 'mark' as a source identification. When that occurs, the conduct of the former owner, by failing to police its mark, can be said to have caused the mark to lose its significance as a mark. However, an owner is not required to act immediately against every possibly infringing use to avoid a holding of abandonment." *Wallpaper Manufacturers, Ltd. v. Crown Wallcovering Corp.*, 680 F.2d 755, 766 (C.C.P.A. 1982).

**Illustrative Case:** *Rossner v. CBS, Inc.*, 612 F. Supp. 334 (S.D.N.Y. 1985)

**The facts:** Plaintiff Judith Rossner wrote a successful novel titled *Looking for Mr. Goodbar*, loosely based on a well-publicized murder of a schoolteacher by a man she picked up in a singles bar. Rossner later sold the movie rights to Paramount Pictures, which duplicated Rossner's success with a film by the same title.

Shortly after the release of Rossner's novel, a *New York Times* reporter wrote two articles and a book respectively titled "Finding Mr. Goodbar," "Finding the Real Mr. Goodbar," and *Closing Time: The True Story of the "Goodbar" Murder*, which reported the actual murder on which Rossner loosely based her novel. Although Rossner knew of the reporter's writing, she decided not to take action because she believed the titles were sufficiently distinguishable from *Looking for Mr. Goodbar*.

As a result of these books and articles, the media began referring to the real murder as the "Goodbar Murder" and the real-life murderer as the "Goodbar Killer." Moreover, swinging singles began using "Goodbar" to refer to elements of the singles scene. As an inevitable consequence of the media attention, CBS produced a two-hour made-for-TV movie about the real murder titled *Trackdown: Finding the Goodbar Killer.*

**The dispute:** The TV movie aired with a disclaimer displayed in a manner unsatisfactory to Rossner. Rossner sued alleging that she conceived of the "Goodbar" moniker and that CBS was attempting to trade off Rossner's reputation and the good will associated with her novel.

In order to prove her case, Rossner needed to first demonstrate that her literary title had achieved "secondary meaning": i.e., that a significant number of people associated "Goodbar" with Rossner's novel alone.

**The ruling:** The court agreed that "Goodbar" was initially associated solely with Rossner's novel. However, due to the movie based on the novel, the journalist's articles and book, and the word's use by swinging singles to describe elements of their lifestyle, the public had associated "Goodbar" with a variety of things other than Rossner's novel:

> First, Rossner sold her rights to the Goodbar title for use in motion pictures to Paramount. Paramount then produced the Goodbar movie and the word "Goodbar" became associated with Paramount and its movie. Second, [Lacey] Fosburgh wrote two articles and a book which prominently used the word "Goodbar" in their titles and identified [John Wayne] Wilson as the "Goodbar Killer." Several newspaper articles reinforced this association in the minds of the public by referring to the [Roseann] Quinn murder as the "Goodbar murder" and to Wilson as the "Goodbar Killer." Finally, the word

itself has been used in the vernacular, specifically, in other movies, television programs and news articles, to identify the "singles' scene," "a dangerous pick-up" or "Mr. Right."

As a result, the court concluded that Rossner could not sustain her cause of action because she failed to prove secondary meaning:

> The strength of the "Goodbar" mark refers to its ability to identify a work sold under the mark as emanating from a particular source, namely, Rossner. Although Rossner is "not required to act immediately against every possibly infringing use [of her mark] to avoid a holding of abandonment," her failure to police the mark has inevitably caused the mark to lose its primary significance as a source-denoting mark. The frequent and disparate uses of the word "Goodbar" in association with Paramount, Fosburgh and the Quinn murder, prevent Rossner from demonstrating secondary meaning in her mark.

## 7. Mind the ®s and ™s

**Rule:** Use the appropriate trademark designation. Trademark owners may not claim that an unregistered mark is registered.

**Rule:** The ® is symbolic of a trademark registered with the appropriate governmental authorities. ™ and ℠ mean that the owner is claiming trademark status, but is not making any claim about registration.

**Rule:** Stating that a mark "is a registered trademark of" an entity is a claim that the trademark is registered with the appropriate governmental authorities. Stating that a mark "is a trademark of" an entity is a claim to trademark status without a claim of registration.

**Rationale:** Claiming registration status where none exists is a fraud on the public. Courts have been unwilling to enforce trademark rights where the owner misrepresented registration status by affixing the ® to an unregistered mark.

**What the courts say:** "The Urecal trademark upon which recovery is sought bears the encircled 'R' symbolic of registration. Plaintiff admits that the mark has never, in fact, been registered. Under these circumstances, the 'clean hands' doctrine, which precludes the grant of relief to one who himself has acted improperly, is applicable. . . . By invoking the doctrine, the court acts to protect the consuming public from commercial dishonesty." *Urecal Corp. v. Masters*, 413 F. Supp. 873 (D. Ill. 1976).

"Finallّy, I find that plaintiffs, whether intentionally or through careless disregard for the significance of such actions, misused the encircled 'R' symbolic of trademark registration and thus are precluded from obtaining the equitable remedy of injunctive relief [stopping defendant from using the mark] under the unclean hands doctrine." *L.F. Gaubert v. Institute of Electrical and Electronics Engineers, Inc.*, 563 F. Supp. 122 (E.D. La. 1983).

**Illustrative Case:** *Fox-Stanley Photo Products, Inc. v. Otaguro*, 339 F. Supp. 1293 (D. Mass. 1972)

**The facts:** Fox-Stanley operated a photo-processing and -supply business under the name Fox Photo, which was printed over a leaping fox. Although Fox-Stanley had never registered "Fox Photo" as a mark with any state agency or the United States Patent and Trademark Office, Fox-Stanley on at least six pieces of advertising collateral placed a circled "R" (®) next to "Fox Photo". Otaguro created a magazine dealing with photography, which he called *FOX*.

**The dispute:** Fox-Stanley sued Otaguro for trademark infringement, alleging that consumers would believe that Fox-Stanley sponsored or was otherwise related to the magazine. In a preliminary hearing, Fox-Stanley asked the court to stop Otaguro from calling the magazine *FOX* until the case could be determined at trial.

**The ruling:** The court regarded Fox-Stanley's misuse of the circle "R" with complete disgust:

> At the hearing plaintiff placed in evidence a number of exhibits. Exhibits 2, 3, 7, 9, 10 and 11 all contain only a purported trade or service mark, consisting of a running red fox with the words "Fox Photo" imprinted thereon. Additionally, the trademark displayed in each of these instances contained the letter "R" surrounded by a circle, which normally and routinely is used to signify the existence of a valid trademark by the party using the trademark. I find that plaintiff does not own a trademark for a running red fox with the words "Fox Photo" imprinted thereon, and that plaintiff has no legal right whatsoever to represent to the public at large, by use of the letter "R" within a circle, that it does own a valid trademark.

The court found that this misrepresentation of trademark status was so serious as to prevent Fox-Stanley from enforcing any trademark rights in "Fox Photo". As a consequence, the court refused to prevent Otaguro from calling the magazine *FOX*:

> It is a familiar principle of equity that a party seeking injunctive relief must come into court with clean hands, and I rule that the illegal use of this trademark by plaintiff by and of itself is a violation of the clean hands doctrine of such a serious magnitude as to disqualify plaintiff from obtaining injunctive relief in this court.

## 8. Play it again, Sam

**Rule:** Use a mark in a consistent manner. Avoid substantial variations on the mark without first considering the legal effect of any changes.

**Rationale:** Enforcing trademark rights ultimately requires the trademark owner to describe the mark and how it is infringed with specificity. If the owner uses the mark inconsistently, then it may be difficult for a court to draft an order preventing future infringement. Furthermore, the U.S. Patent and Trademark Office may register a mark to look, sound, and read a certain way. A granted registration can often consist of words, colors, and graphics. Altering an existing mark may make it inconsistent with the registration and can confuse the public as to the actual trademark.

**What the courts say:** "While a mark can obviously be 'modified' out of existence, minor changes in a registered mark do not constitute abandonment. The law seems clear that as long as the new mark is closely related to the old, the old mark's registration protects the new one as well." *Li'l Red Barn, Inc. v. Red Barn System, Inc.*, 322 F. Supp. 98, 107-08 (D. Ind. 1970).

**Illustrative Case:** *Ilco Corp. v. Ideal Security Hardware Corp.*, 527 F.2d 1221 (C.C.P.A. 1976)

**The facts:** Ilco and Ideal both sold security tool display racks to hardware stores with the words "Home Protection Center" posted across the top of the rack. Ideal first marketed the racks as early as 1965 with the words "Home Protection Center" posted across the racks, and in 1970 changed the designation to "Home Protection Center". Ilco began marketing the racks with the "Home Protection Center" posting in 1967.

**The dispute:** Ilco attempted to register the mark "Home Protection Center" with the United States Patent and Trademark Office. Ideal filed an action with the USPTO attempting to cancel the registration based on Ideal's prior use of the mark "Home Protection Hardware". The issue was which entity first used the "Home Protection Center" mark. The USPTO found for Ideal on the theory that Ideal's prior use of "Home Protection Hardware" extended to the "Home Protection Center" mark because the change in the mark did not alter its distinguishing characteristics. Ilco appealed to the Court of Customs and Patent Appeals.

**The ruling:** The court reversed the USPTO and allowed Ilco to register the mark because it found that Ideal's original mark did not have the same distinguishing characteristics as "Home Protection Center". The court first acknowledged that marks can change over time without being lost:

> The law permits a user who changes the form of its mark to retain the benefit of its use of the earlier form, without abandonment, if the new and old forms create the same, continuing commercial impression. . . . The only requirement in these instances is that the mark be modified in such a fashion as to retain its trademark impact and symbolize a single and continuing commercial impression. That is, a change that does not alter its distinctive characteristics represents a continuity of trademark rights. Thus, where the distinctive character of the mark is not changed, the mark is, in effect, the same and the rights obtained by virtue of the earlier use of the prior form inure to the later form.

The court did not accept, however, that "Home Protection Hardware" was part of a continuing commercial impression with "Home Protection Center":

> The test to be applied here is whether "Home Protection Hardware" and "Home Protection Center" create the same, continuing commercial impression. . . . In our opinion appellee is not entitled to rely on its use of "Home Protection Hardware" because it creates a different commercial impression than "Home Protection Center", when the marks are applied to the goods [which are the tool racks, not the tools themselves]. That appellee may have used them interchangeably is not material because commercial impression is gauged by the impact on the public, in this case hardware store operators and their customers. "Home Protection Center" signifies a unitary aggregation of goods related to home protection, the one place in the hardware store

to go for home protection needs. "Home Protection Hardware" . . . refer[s] to the hardware itself and not to its collection in one place on the display rack.

As a result, the court denied Ideal the right to rely on its first use of "Home Protection Hardware" in establishing who first used the mark. Thus the court found that Ilco had a right to register "Home Protection Center" because it was the first entity to use the mark in association with the display racks.

## Rules for using the brand in text

The following rules apply when using the mark in a sentence (in an advertisement, for example) or as part of a larger textual presentation (such as a business card or stationary), as opposed to using the mark by itself.

### 1. Don't let the mark stand alone

**Rule:** When using the mark in a sentence, always use the mark as an adjective to modify a noun. Never use the mark as a noun or a verb.

**Rationale:** Trademarks identify the source of products; they do not describe the products themselves. Once the public begins to refer to a product by the trademark alone, the mark has become generic and cannot receive trademark protection. Using the mark as a noun or a verb teaches the public to refer to the product by the mark alone instead of by its generic name. Because adjectives modify nouns, using the mark as an adjective teaches the public that the mark is the product's source, e.g., "a 'Ford' pick-up truck" or "a cup of 'Starbucks' coffee."

**Examples:**

*WRONG*:

Nothing comes between me and my "Calvins."

You can "Mimeograph" a document in no time.

Pick up some "Cube Steaks" at your local grocer.

Nothing burns brighter than "Kerosene."

*RIGHT*:

>Nothing comes between me and my "Calvin Klein" jeans.

>You can make a "Mimeograph" copy of a document in no time.

>Pick up some "Cube Steak" tenderized beef patties at your local grocer.

>Nothing burns brighter than "Kerosene" fuel.

**What the courts say:** Bayer "used the word 'Aspirin' as though it was a general term […] The most striking part of the label read, 'Bayer—Tablets of Aspirin.' [This] show[s] how the plaintiff itself recognized the meaning which the word had acquired, because the phrase most properly means that these tablets were Bayer's make of the drug known as 'Aspirin.' It presupposes that the persons reached were using the word to denote a kind of product. Were it not so, why the addition of 'Bayer,' and especially why the significant word 'of'?" *Bayer Co. v. United Drug Co.*, 272 F. 505 (S.D.N.Y. 1921) (L. Hand, J.).

**Illustrative Case:** *America Online, Inc. v. AT&T Corp.*, 64 F. Supp. 2d 549 (E.D. Va. 1999), *aff'd in part and rev'd in part*, 243 F.3d 812 (4th Cir. 2001)

**The facts:** AOL asserted trademark protection for "IM" to denote the instant messaging feature on its America Online Internet service. AT&T started using "IM" for the same purpose. AOL sued AT&T for trademark infringement.

**The dispute:** AOL asserted that "IM" was an AOL trademark. AT&T countered that "IM" was simply an initialism for "instant messaging," which described the service and did not deserve trademark protection.

**The ruling:** The court found that "IM" was an initialism for "instant messaging." In reaching this conclusion, the court relied in part on AOL employees' use of the term "IM":

>[T]he Court has little trouble determining that IM is

generic and not protected by [trademark law]. The record indicates that AOL and AOL employees frequently use IM in a manner which indicates that it is a noun, not an adjective (an AOL employee stating "…the letters IM…blinked to let them know that they had an IM pending"; in an article, an AOL spokesperson said: "We'll say, 'I IM'ed him, but he never called back'; or, 'Stop IM'ing me, I'm trying to work' . . . [IM] has become part of the vocabulary"…).

## 2. Make the mark stand out in the crowd

**Rule:** Distinguish the mark from the remaining text. Use some method of alerting the reader that they are seeing a mark instead of an ordinary word.

**Rationale:** If the trademark owner fails to alert the public that a word has trademark significance, then the public has no way of knowing that the word is a mark for the product instead of the product name.

**Examples:**

*All capitals:*

Purchase a package of TRADEMARK products today.

*The trademark designations:*

Purchase a package of Trademark™ products today.

Purchase a package of Trademark$^{SM}$ products today.

Purchase a package of Registered Trademark® products today.

*Unusual spacing or capitals:*

Purchase a package of TradeMARK products today.

Purchase a package of RegisteredTrademark products today.

*Bolding, underlining, or italicizing all or part of a mark:*

Purchase a package of Trade**mark** products today.

Purchase a package of <u>Trademark</u> products today.

Purchase a package of Trade*mark* products today.

*Quotation marks:*

> Purchase a package of "'Trademark" products today.

**What the courts say:** "Unless attention is drawn to the particular word or term as being indicative of source of origin of that product, the term is not being used as a trademark." *Wonder Labs, Inc. v. Procter & Gamble Co.*, 728 F. Supp. 1058 (S.D.N.Y. 1990).

"At times, plaintiff has capitalized and printed the word 'delite'; at other times, it has used script form and small letters. [. . .] From this use, it might at trial be held that the word 'Delite' was not being used in a trademark sense but in a descriptive sense—to describe what was a juice product—and that this description varied according to the need or whim of plaintiff." *Sunrise Home Juices, Inc. v. Coca Cola Co.*, 220 F. Supp. 558 (S.D.N.Y. 1963).

**Illustrative Case:** *Birtcher Electro Medical Systems, Inc. v. Beacon Laboratories, Inc.*, 738 F. Supp. 417 (D. Colo. 1990)

**The facts:** Birtcher manufactured a medical device used to promote blood coagulation around an incision during surgery, which it referred to at various times as the "Argon Beam Coagulator," "ABC," "System 6000," and "Beam." Beacon manufactured a similar device, which it called "Beamer One," and at times referred to it as an "Argon Beam Coagulator."

**The dispute:** Birtcher sued Beacon for trademark infringement and brought a motion requesting the court to prevent Beacon from describing the device with the word "Beam" or any similar word until the court could fully try the case. Beacon argued that "Argon Beam Coagulator" and "Beam" were not trademarks.

**The ruling:** The court found that Birtcher did not use the terms "Argon Beam Coagulator" or "Beam" as trademarks. In reviewing Birtcher's promotional literature, the court noted that Birtcher frequently used the terms as a noun as opposed to an adjective:

Beacon showed numerous instances in which Birtcher literature and videotaped advertising used the terms as nouns as opposed to adjectives, indicating that the terms were generic labels for the product itself. For example, in a document authored by Birtcher for a direct mailing campaign to approximately 30,000 surgeons, Birtcher described its device as the "Bard® ABC™ Argon Beam Coagulator."

Furthermore, Birtcher failed to distinguish the words "Beam" and "Argon Beam Coagulator" from other words that were not trademarks:

[M]uch of the literature prepared by Birtcher used the terms as nouns and none of the publicly disseminated literature designates the terms as trademarks by using a "TM" signal. Notably, there were examples of documents, which were being drafted for public release, that designated "Argon Beam Coagulator" as a trademark by using the "TM" symbol. However, before releasing the documents to the public, Birtcher removed the trademark designation. [. . .]

Birtcher typically capitalized the initial letters in the phrases "Argon Beam Coagulator" and "Argon Beam," and occasionally the term "Beam." However, Beacon presented numerous examples of other phrases which Birtcher indiscriminately had capitalized initial letters but to which Birtcher claimed no trademark protection. Beacon established that Birtcher never intended to use the terms as trademarks and only rarely used them as trademarks. Thus, the consuming public is unlikely to have interpreted the terms as indications of the product's source.

As a result, the court refused to prevent Beacon from using the words "Beam" or the phrase "Argon Beam Coagulator" in describing the device because the court believed that Birtcher would be unlikely to prove at trial that the word and phrase were trademarks.

### 3. Don't give the mark an identity crisis

**Rule:** When the mark is similar to the company name (e.g., "Acme, Inc." uses the mark "Acme"), do not use the mark to refer to the company name. Similarly, do not use the company name as the mark.

**Rationale:** Company names are nouns. Trademarks can never be used as nouns. When referring to Acme, Incorporated as Acme, use normal text, and do not use the registration symbol.

**Examples:**

*WRONG:*

Acme® has the world's most diverse product line.

ACME has the world's most diverse product line.

*Acme* has the world's most diverse product line.

The Acme®, Inc. product line is the most diverse in the world.

*RIGHT:*

Acme has the world's most diverse product line.

Acme, Inc. has the world's most diverse product line.

The Acme® product line is the most diverse in the world.

The ACME product line is the most diverse in the world.

The Acme, Inc. product line is the most diverse in the world.

The Acme product line is the most diverse in the world.

NOTE: The final two uses are trade name uses. In the final four sentences, either the trademark or the trade name is appropriate. This is an instance where trademarks and trade names overlap.

**What the courts say:** "Throughout this litigation, the parties have indiscriminately referred to the word as a trademark, service mark, and trade name. Each category indicates a different use of a word: a trademark identifies and distinguishes a product, a service mark a service, and a trade name a business. Use of a word may fall within more than one category; indeed, as a practical matter distinctions between use in one category and use in another may be difficult to make. The category in which use of a word falls may, however, at times determine the protection accorded the use. Trade names, for example, though protected at common law, cannot be registered under and are not protected by the [federal trademark statute]." *Safeway Stores, Inc. v. Safeway Discount Drugs, Inc.*, 675 F.2d 1160, 1162 (11th Cir. 1982).

"...the inference is created by the addition of the address 'Floydada, Texas' to the placard that the use here involved does not so much distinguish appellant's cattle as it identifies appellant as the source of the shipment while the crate and its contents are in transit. That is trade name usage as distinguished from trademark usage." *In re Lyndale Farm*, 186 F.2d 723 (C.C.P.A. 1951).

**Illustrative Case:** *Application of Walker Process Equipment, Inc.*, 233 F.2d 329 (C.C.P.A. 1956)

**The facts:** Walker sought to register "Walker Process Equipment, Inc." as a trademark with the predecessor to the United States Patent and Trademark Office. Walker submitted samples of use that contained the word "Proquip" in large letters, and the words "Walker Process Equipment, Inc." appearing over the words "Aurora Illinois" or "Aurora Ill. U.S.A." A trademark examiner and the assistant commissioner of patents refused the registration because they found that Walker did not use the proposed mark as a trademark.

**The dispute:** Walker appealed the assistant commissioner of patents' decision to the Court of Customs and Patent Appeals, arguing that "Walker Process Equipment, Inc." was a trademark.

**The ruling:** The court upheld the assistant commissioner patents' decision, finding that Walker did not use the proposed mark as a trademark, only as a trade name. The court began by discussing the distinction between trademarks and trade names. While it conceded that the two might overlap, it noted that a distinction generally exists between trade names and trademarks:

> The issue is whether the use of the words "Walker Process Equipment Inc." in the described manner constitutes use as a trade-mark, or, as held by the Patent Office tribunals, the words are merely a trade name used as such. The distinction between trade-marks and trade names is not always clear. . . . the two terms may sometimes overlap, but, generally speaking, a trade-mark is applicable to a vendible commodity and a trade name to a business.

Although the proposed mark was originally a trade name, the court noted that this alone did not prevent registration so long as Walker used the proposed mark to distinguish the source of its goods as well as the name of its business:

> There can be no doubt that the words "Walker Process Equipment Inc." constitute a trade name, but that, in itself, would not necessarily preclude them from being a trade-mark as well since . . . the name of a corporation may be a trade-mark, a trade name, or both. . . . Since the words "Walker Process Equipment Inc." were not adopted to identify or distinguish goods, and would not, standing alone, be considered a trade-mark, any trade-mark significance which they might have must be of a secondary nature acquired as the result of use. It is therefore necessary to further examine how those words were used.

The court found that Walker's samples of use did not establish that Walker used the proposed mark as a trademark because Walker enlarged the mark "Proquip" and not the proposed mark.

Furthermore, Walker included the address in close proximity to the proposed mark. These aspects of Walker's sample indicated that the proposed mark was a trade name rather than a trademark:

> [T]he specimens submitted by appellant show that the words "Walker Process Equipment Inc." are used in association with the words "Aurora Illinois" or "Aurora Ill. U.S.A." and with the trade-mark "Proquip," which is more prominently displayed than the other words. Since the word "Proquip" is a trade-mark, it must necessarily identify and distinguish the goods to which it is applied, and being the most prominent feature of the specimens presented, it is obviously intended to be the principal means of identification. The words "Walker Process Equipment Inc." are therefore clearly unnecessary so far as any trade-mark purpose is concerned, since the goods are sufficiently identified without them by an arbitrary word which would normally be considered to be a trade-mark. While it may be that two or more distinct trade-marks may be applied simultaneously to the same goods, that is clearly not the usual practice, and where, as here, the most prominent feature of a label is a word which is unquestionably a trade-mark, the natural inference would be that the remaining words on the label are not to be considered a trade-mark.
>
> Moreover, in the instant case, each of the specimens includes the words 'Aurora Illinois' or 'Aurora Ill. U.S.A.' displayed in such a manner as to make it clear they indicate the location of Walker Process Equipment Inc. . . . [T]he addition of the address of Walker Process Equipment Inc. suggests that the name of the corporation is not being used as a trade-mark.

### 4. Don't let the mark lose its way home

**Rule:** When using a company domain name or address as a mark, do not use the mark as a domain name or address. Do not make directional information appear like a mark, and do not make the mark appear like directional information.

**Rationale:** Addresses and domain names generally cannot function as trademarks because they identify where to find the addressee, they do not identify a source of goods. Distinguishing the use from other directional information will increase the probability that the domain name will function as a trademark.

**Examples:**

*WRONG*:

View our full line of products at ACME.COM®.

View our full line of products at ACME.COM.

You can find SAKS on FIFTH AVENUE, New York.

SAKS, Fifth Avenue, New York, NY.

*RIGHT*:

View our full line of products at <u>www.acme.com</u>.

View our full line of products at <u>acme.com</u>.

View our full line of products at our ACME.COM® online purchasing center.

You can find our SAKS FIFTH AVENUE store at 611 Fifth Avenue, New York.

**Note:** <u>www.acme.com</u> is distinguished from the remaining text, which traditionally would indicate a trademark usage. Because hyperlinks are also distinguished from remaining text, the public should recognize that this is a hyperlink use, not a trademark use.

**What the USPTO says:** "By analogy with the registration of trade names, the more distinctive the presentation of the internet domain name and the further it is physically removed from other informational data appearing on the specimen, the more likely the name will be perceived to function as a service mark." *PTO Policy Statement: Trademark Examination of Domain Names and Classification of Computer Related Goods and Services*, January 1998.

**Illustrative Case:** *In re Eilberg*, 49 U.S.P.Q.2d 1955 (T.T.A.B. 1998)

**The facts:** Attorney Eilberg wanted to register his domain name www.eilberg.com as a trademark. His samples of use showed that he placed the domain name on the lower right-hand portion of his business cards and letterhead.

**The dispute:** The USPTO refused registration, and Eilberg appealed the decision to the Trademark Trial and Appeals Board.

**The ruling:** The TTAB found that the domain name did not function as a trademark:

> As shown, the asserted mark identifies applicant's Internet domain name, by use of which one can access applicant's Web site. In other words, the asserted mark www.eilberg.com merely indicates the location on the Internet where applicant's Web site appears. It does not separately identify applicant's legal services as such.

The TTAB conceded, however, that the domain name could obtain trademark status if used appropriately:

> ...if applicant's law firm name were, say, eilberg.com and were presented prominently on applicant's letterheads and business cards as the name under which applicant was rendering its legal services, then that mark may well be registrable.

# PART III

## Tricks of the Trade: The Practical Side of Brand Protection Programs

### How To Create Your Own Legally Enforceable Brand

Creating a brand is one of the most challenging and rewarding opportunities in business. This is because a brand must convey your product's values in a simple, easily recognizable way. To use an example with which I am familiar, I always believed the "AmericanAirlines" brand primarily stood for the following principals:

- Competence
- Safety
- Professionalism
- Travel
- Adventure
- Freedom
- Reunion
- Strength
- Comfort
- Reliability
- Patriotism
- Innovation

I also believed that the "AmericanAirlines" and "AA" brand conveyed these virtues through the words "American" and "Airlines," the color scheme and font, and the famous scissor eagle as the corporate mascot flying between two "As." American cemented these principals in consumer minds through advertising, literature, programs, and, most importantly, the consumer's experience in using American's service.

In creating your own brand, an intelligent first step is to make a simplified list of your product's core values. Once you have made this list, it will be easier to determine if the brand you choose will convey these values to consumers. Consultants, focus groups, and advertising agencies can help you develop a word, phrase, or other symbol that effectively conveys your product's core values. The process does not stop there, however. In fact, the most important work has not yet taken place.

Once you have picked a potential brand, you must then make sure it has the potential to have value. To have any value, your brand must have two characteristics: 1) it must readily associate the product with a single source; and 2) it must be exclusive to your company. Marketing and legal principals form the basis for these requirements.

From the marketing standpoint, a brand serves no purpose if consumers associate it with another company or with the industry generally. Likewise, spending money promoting a brand that a competitor can start using forfeits any competitive advantage obtained by promoting the brand.

From a legal standpoint, a brand must associate a product with its source or the brand is no longer enforceable. Furthermore, enforceability of a brand's exclusivity in court depends upon its trademark status. If your brand is not a trademark, then anyone can use it. It would be pretty stupid to pour millions of dollars into promoting a "brand" that a competitor can use, but companies have done it over and over again.

As an obvious example, a producer of automobiles could not use "car" as a trademark for its products. First, "car" is a generic term that consumers associate with automobiles made by anyone, anywhere, not one company. Second, no court is going to stop other automobile makers from using the term "car" to promote their products.

Thus, avoid using a generic or industry term as a brand. It cannot be exclusive to your company and thus will have little value. Of course, the example I give above—the "AmericanAirlines" brand—seems to fly in the face of this statement. The "AmericanAirlines" brand, however, is called a "composite" mark. When used together, the phrase "AmericanAirlines" creates a commercial impression distinct from each word used alone. Thus, "Coca-Cola" can use the generic word "cola" as part of its mark.

Furthermore, American's brand developed over many years of continued use and promotion. It has achieved what the courts call "secondary meaning." In other words, consumers associate the phrase "American Airlines" with a single company, not with any airline in America or, for that matter, with any other company, period.

Finally, the phrase "American Airlines" was never descriptive of an airline in America any more than the phrase "United Airlines" described a unified airline, "U.S. Airways" described an airline in the U.S., or "Continental Airlines" described an airline that served a continent.

In contrast, in 1925, Skinner Manufacturing Company created a cereal made of bran and raisins. It marketed this product under the mark "Raisin Bran." No other company marketed a similar product until 1942, and for nearly twenty years, Skinner did "all that could be done to appropriate 'Raisin-BRAN' as the trade-mark of its product," including obtaining federal registration for "Raisin Bran" as a trademark and clearly associating the term "Raisin Bran" in the consumer's mind as a symbol for Skinner's product.

In 1942, however, Kellogg Sales Company and General Foods Sales Company entered the market by also selling bran cereals with raisins, and they also called the product "Raisin Bran." Skinner sued, and the court refused to prevent Kellogg and General Foods from using the term "Raisin Bran" to describe their product. Essentially, the mark was doomed from the start. As the court observed, even doing everything right could not make an exclusive trademark out of the name of a product: "Whatever the trade name 'Raisin-BRAN' may have meant prior to the advent of [the] competing products, it is a reasonable conclusion that the words 'raisin bran' have at all times meant bran with raisins in it." *Skinner Manufacturing Co. v. Kellogg Sales Co.*, 143 F.2d 895 (8th Cir. 1944).

It helps in developing a brand to understand the basic different types of trademarks and the strength that courts will accord these marks. The strongest marks are "fanciful" marks that have been invented solely to function as trademarks. Examples include "Xerox" and "Polaroid."

Although courts accord fanciful marks the strongest degree of protection, fanciful marks also suffer from the disadvantage of being the marks most susceptible to misuse. This is because if not used properly, the public comes to associate this new word with the product itself instead of the product's source. Many people have substituted the word "Xerox" for "copy," and the word "Polaroid" for "photograph." If too many people do this and the trademark owner fails to take steps to educate the public, then the trademark can become an ordinary word, and courts will not enforce its trademark status. For example, the words "aspirin" and "cellophane" started as fanciful marks and were lost due to the trademark owner encouraging the public to use the mark as the name of the product.

The second strongest marks are "arbitrary" marks—symbols in common use that were not previously associated with the mark owner's product. For example, "Apple" computers, "Camel" cigarettes, and "Indian" motorcycles represent common words that have become associated with certain products only through trademark use. Likewise, stars, stripes, and check marks are in common use, but Converse, Adidas, and Nike associated them with athletic shoes.

Arbitrary marks come with a natural protection against misuse: because the public already associates the word with something else, the trademark owner and the public are less likely to use the mark as the sole name for the product. For example, if someone said "I'm going to ride my Indian," then most people would get a little uncomfortable instead of understanding that the person was going to ride a motorcycle. Consequently, arbitrary marks are more likely to be used in association with the product, thus retaining the trademark status and protecting the mark owner against misuse.

Courts give the next highest degree of protection to "suggestive" marks, which suggest a product's attribute but do not directly describe the product. For example, "Atlas" van lines, "Coppertone" tanning lotion, and "Husky" tools represent words that suggest an aspect of a product—strength, dark skin, and durability, respectively—without directly describing it.

Courts afford the lowest degree of trademark protection to "descriptive" marks, which directly describe a product or its attribute(s). These marks fall short of being generic words for the product, however. Creating trademark significance for descriptive terms requires educating consumers as to their trademark significance. This generally requires significant advertising expenditures, and, if suing to enforce the mark, significant costs in terms of legal fees and expert analysis and testimony to prove that the mark has attained secondary meaning in the minds of consumers. Expenses for pursuing such a case through trial would almost certainly exceed $150,000 and would most likely double or even triple that amount. Moreover, descriptive marks are more likely to end up in litigation because they are more likely to be infringed, and it is also more likely that the infringer will refuse to stop using the mark, forcing a court to decide the issue. Thus, unless you have a significant budget for advertising and trademark enforcement, avoid adopting descriptive marks.

Two other problems arise from adopting descriptive marks. First, establishing secondary meaning provides no room for error—using the word in its descriptive sense can be fatal to establishing its trademark meaning. Second, only in rare instances can the owner of a descriptive mark monopolize the word. With newer marks, the best a descriptive mark owner can generally do is force a competitor to clearly disclose his product's source when using the descriptive term.

Other marks that are subject to the same problems as descriptive marks include marks that incorporate geography, personal names, titles of single literary works, descriptive titles of a literary series, and any other packaging, product shapes, designs, or symbols that are not inherently distinctive. In fact, the USPTO generally will not register marks that are:

- used primarily as trade names (the name of a business);
- purely decorative (ornamental). For example, the "Polo Player" logo on a "Polo" shirt identifies the source and is a trademark, but the collar on the shirt is purely decorative and does not identify the source absent a showing that the public sees the collar as indicating the shirt comes from Polo Ralph Lauren Corporation;
- purely informational. For example, "Drive Safely" cannot be a mark for "Volvo" cars because this is an instruction rather than an identifier of Volvo's products;
- a product's color, without proving the color of the product indicates its source. For example, Owens-Corning was able to register the color pink for insulation by showing that the public associated pink insulation with Owens-Corning;
- names of artists or authors;
- titles of single literary works;
- grade, model, or style designations within a product line, without proving the designation indicates the product's source;
- design backgrounds and shapes always used in conjunction with a mark but without independent source identifying significance;
- names given to live plants or agricultural seeds. Here the USPTO makes the determination if the name is generic for that type of plant or if it indicates that type of plant coming from a particular source;
- purely functional scents. For example, perfume scents are generally not registerable, but the USPTO has allowed registration of a scent given to yarn;
- government insignias;
- names, portraits or signatures of a particular living person without his or her consent or deceased United States presidents dur-

ing his or her spouse's life without consent of the spouse;

- primarily surnames ("King," while a surname, has other connotations, while "Jones" is primarily a surname);

Although a brand ideally will be associated with your company specifically, this is not a legal requirement. For trademark protection, a brand need only be associated with a single, albeit anonymous, source. As one court noted in rejecting the argument that the public had to know the product's actual maker for trademark protection:

> Of course there may not be one in a hundred buyers who knows that [the trademarked whiskey] is made by Buchanan or wholesaled by Fleischmann. Probably all that such buyers know is that BLACK & WHITE Scotch whiskey has satisfied them in the past or that they have heard of it and the average purchaser would no doubt select for the use of his guests something with which he was familiar and thus purchase BLACK & WHITE Whiskey. What are we to say about the same purchaser who starts for home on a hot evening and decides to take home beer for refreshment? He stops at Ralph's and notes beer bearing the label BLACK & WHITE in that store's stock. We think it plain that the likelihood of confusion and mistake is present here.

*Fleischmann Distilling Corp. v. Maier Brewing Co.*, 314 F.2d 149 (9th Cir.), *cert. denied*, 374 U.S. 830 (1963). From a marketing standpoint, however, it often adds value to have the public associate your brand with your company instead of "a single, albeit anonymous, source." Such an association can lead to cross-marketing opportunities as well as a transfer of consumer good will between product lines.

Once you have decided on a brand, the next step is to make sure your use of the brand will not infringe on someone else's trademark. Making this determination requires legal skill and judgments not teachable in a single text, particularly of this length. Thus, you should seek professional assistance in determining whether your mark will subject you to infringement liability.

You can do things that help you make a judgment for yourself as to infringement, but it would be a mistake to draw your own conclusion about infringement liability based on these exercises. First, visit the United States Patent and Trademark Office Web site at *www.uspto.gov*, and perform a Boolean search to see if anyone has registered your proposed mark. Second, use Web search engines to see if someone is using the mark, but has not yet registered it. If you find that someone else is using the mark or has registered it, this does not necessarily preclude your using the mark. Whether you can use the mark as well depends on whether your use of the mark is confusingly similar to the senior user's mark.

Once a legal professional has cleared your mark for use, the next step is to begin using the mark in commerce. Trademark rights cannot be hoarded. Although the USPTO has a procedure called an intent to use application that allows you to, in essence, "reserve" a mark for a limited period of time, you cannot do so indefinitely and must eventually start using the mark.

Once you have started using the mark in commerce, you should make a determination as to whether you want to register the mark. Registration takes time, so in general, it makes sense to register marks you intend to use for a long time and avoid registering marks that you are using for a one-time promotion. If the one-time promotion turns into a lifetime commitment, you can always register the mark later as no time limit exists on how long you can use a mark before filing a registration application.

**Tips on creating a brand:**

1. Make a list of your product's core values.

2. Develop a word, phrase, or other symbol that conveys these core values.

3. Determine whether your brand is a strong or weak trademark, and understand the implications this can have on your use of the brand.

4. Make sure that no one else is already using your brand.

5. Begin using your brand. Notify the public that it is a trademark or service mark by placing a ™ next to it (if you are using the brand for goods) or an ^SM next to it (if you are using the brand for services). Also place the following language on material using the brand: "[Insert brand] is a trademark of [insert your company name]" (if you are using the brand for goods); or "[Insert brand] is a service mark of [insert your company name]" (if you are using the brand for services).

6. Record the date you first used the brand, and keep a file containing a sample of each use along with the date and time of publication.

7. Decide if you want to register your brand. *Never, ever* place an "®" next to an unregistered brand. *Never, ever* refer to an unregistered brand with the words "[Insert brand] is a *registered* trademark of [insert your company name]."

# Create an Overall Brand Strategy

To protect a brand effectively, you must know what the brand represents. After you have created a list of core values in selecting a brand, retain that list and revise it as the brand evolves. This list should govern the overall promotion and protection of the brand.

Ideally, a brand should reflect all the characteristics of a company's goods or services. Thus, a brand strategy should incorporate those characteristics into every aspect of the company. Every employee and owner should endeavor to promote the brand through positive relationships with consumers.

Southwest Airlines provides an excellent example of a coordinated brand strategy. Southwest "began with one simple notion: If you get your passengers to their destinations when they want to get there, on time, at the lowest possible fares, and make darn sure they have a good time doing it, people will fly your airline." That beginning transformed into a mission: "dedication to the highest quality of Customer Service delivered with a sense of warmth, friendliness, individual pride, and Company Spirit."

Other excerpts from Southwest's Web site demonstrate how Southwest integrates that mission into numerous aspects of its overall operation:

> Southwest Airlines Co. ("Southwest") is a major domestic airline that provides primarily shorthaul, high-frequency, point-to-point, low-fare service. [. . .] Southwest has the lowest operating cost structure in the domestic airline industry and consistently offers the lowest and simplest fares. Southwest also has one of the best overall Customer Service records. LUV is our stock exchange symbol, selected to represent our home at Dallas Love Field, as well as the theme of our Employee and Customer relationships. [. . .]
>
> We've also got more than 355 of the newest jets in the nation, with an average age of 8.75 years. Included in our fleet are three flying killer whales, Shamu One, Two and

Three; Lone Star One, painted like the Texas flag, to celebrate Southwest Airlines' 20th Anniversary in a style and
manner second to none; Arizona One, a symbol of the
importance of the state of Arizona to Southwest Airlines;
California One, a high-flying tribute to the state of California;
Silver One, our 25th Anniversary plane; Triple Crown One,
dedicated to the Employees of Southwest Airlines for their
marvelous achievement of five consecutive annual Triple
Crown awards; Nevada One, a high-flying tribute to the state
of Nevada; and the newest member of the family—New
Mexico One, also known as Zia, painted in the bright yellow
of the New Mexico flag.

In May 1988, we were the first airline to win the coveted
Triple Crown for a month—Best On-time Record, Best
Baggage Handling, and Fewest Customer Complaints. Since
then we've won it more than thirty times, as well as five
annual Triple Crowns for 1992, 1993, 1994, 1995, and 1996.
And no other airline has contributed more to the advance-
ment of the commercial airline industry. We were the first
airline with a frequent flyer program to give credit for the
number of trips taken and not the number of miles flown.
We also pioneered senior discounts, Fun Fares, Fun Packs, a
same-day air freight delivery service, ticketless travel, and
many other unique programs.

Southwest's brand image starts at the top. For example, I once
observed Southwest's CEO joyfully handing out peanuts to passengers. In doing so, he set a tone for employees to emulate and customers to admire. To his customers, his actions said, "You're important to me." To the employees on board, his actions said, "Your job is
important, and I'm pitching in to help." His actions were consistent
with Southwest's fun, low-fare, "we care" brand and were a good
example of setting a tone of integrating brand strategy into every
part of the company's operation.

Although every employee should endeavor to *promote* the brand, every employee should not *control* the brand. An important step in protecting the brand is limiting control of the brand. One cannot read this book's preceding sections without understanding how easily mismanagement can destroy a brand. Placing the brand in the hands of a few people responsible for its management can insulate the brand from misuse.

For example, say a shipping company headquartered in Phoenix has more than 100,000 employees in numerous locations. Fred, a supplies manager in Tulsa who orders pens and other giveaways sporting the company brand, makes a deal with his Uncle Jim that allows Jim to place the company brand on a fleet of toy trucks for resale under license. Fred never monitors Uncle Jim's use of the brand and never gets Uncle Jim to sign a contract protecting the mark.

Two years later, Fred's supervisor learns about the deal and insists that Jim stop producing the toys. Jim says talk to my attorney. Fred gave me permission, never got a written contract, and never monitored my use of the mark. The company gave me a naked license. The company abandoned the brand.

Is Jim right? Fred had the authority as supplies manager to order branded products. The company had nothing in place to insulate the brand from Fred's mismanagement. Jim has a decent chance of winning his case and taking control of the brand, at least for the purpose of placing it on toys.

A large company with numerous employees in different locations is susceptible to this scenario. A company can best avoid it by limiting the brand's ownership in a way that prevents even well-intentioned employees from taking control of the brand. One method of limiting ownership is to create a holding company that owns the brand. The holding company then licenses the brand back to the company. Under such a licensing arrangement, the brand owner could argue that Fred could not have granted a naked license to Jim because Fred does not represent the brand's owner: He is merely a licensee's agent.

This licensing arrangement can also provide certain state tax benefits. Tax benefits should not be the primary motivation for setting up a holding company to own the brand, however. Companies that use this strategy solely for tax purposes miss an opportunity to protect one of their most valuable assets.

Brand owners should also create internal policies that protect the brand from misuse. Companies should tailor these policies to match the company culture. For example, written policies work fairly well in regulated industries where employees tend to work by the book, but may not work well in companies where employees view regulations and limitations on authority as encroachments on artistic freedom or deal killers.

Policies to protect the brand can include the following:

- restricting employee authority to use, license, or alter the brand without approval;
- creating a brand standards committee or trademark czar to monitor and approve brand use;
- limiting the number of vendors that provide branded products to the company;
- standardizing contracts to protect brand use;
- establishing a licensing program;
- requiring employee education on brand use;
- requiring employees and vendors to obtain copies of company trademarks from a single source.

A brand owner should also adopt a brand standards manual that describes the proper use of the brand. The brand standards manual should be easily accessible (an intranet site is ideal) and provide downloadable or camera-ready samples of the brand.

Brand owners can best ensure that employees will follow these policies by providing access to trademark samples at a single source that also educates and warns employees about the consequences of misusing the brand. Intranet or Internet sites can be set up to require passwords for access, and password approval can come with instructions on use. The Web site can require an educational session or a click agreement to use the brand in accordance with the brand standards manual before providing users access to downloadable brand images. The Web site can also record who accessed and downloaded the brand and for what purpose. Companies can use this Web-based brand access system as part of an overall brand monitoring strategy.

The downside of the single source approach is that employees without access will simply create their own versions of the mark. While this lack of consistency can damage the mark, the damage inflicted by uneducated use generally outweighs the damage inflicted by bootleg copies.

Tips on integrating legal protection programs into the overall brand strategy:

1. Educate employees on brand integration along with brand protection.

2. Limit ownership of the brand through a holding company to insulate the brand from misuse.

3. Limit authority to approve use, licensing, and alteration of the brand by creating either a trademark czar or brand standards committee to oversee such activities.

4. Create a single source for accessing downloadable reproductions of the brand that educates employees on use policies and the consequences of misuse.

# Using It to Avoid Losing It

In 1986, Trans World Airlines under Carl Icahn acquired Ozark Airlines and began merging Ozark into TWA's operations. TWA painted over the Ozark planes and, in effect, stamped out the "Ozark Airlines" brand in favor of TWA. Once TWA had fully absorbed Ozark, a new Ozark Airlines formed, utilizing the same name, and trademarks similar to the "Ozark Airlines" marks TWA had purchased. TWA paid money for the "Ozark Airlines" brand and the good will it represented. But because TWA failed to use the "Ozark Airlines" trademarks in commerce, TWA lost all rights to the "Ozark Airlines" brand. Worse yet, a new competitive airline flying some of the old Ozark Airlines routes inherited the good will that the original Ozark Airlines had built up over many years.

TWA lost the right to use the "Ozark Airlines" brand because TWA failed to use it. TWA should have either sold the "Ozark Airlines" trademarks or figured out a way to keep the "Ozark Airlines" brand alive through continued use. By letting its rights to the "Ozark Airlines" brand die, TWA effectively gave a start up competitor several million dollars in free advertising, good will, and instant name recognition.

To prevent the loss of the "Ozark Airlines" brand, TWA needed to use the brand in commerce. TWA could have done this by flying a fleet of "Ozark Airlines" branded or co-branded planes in recognition of Ozark Airlines' proud history and as a tribute to the Ozark Airlines employees and customers who came to TWA as part of the acquisition. TWA could also have kept the brand alive through an active licensing program creating goods or services marketed under the "Ozark Airlines" brand.

Of course, a company cannot maintain a brand simply for the purpose of hoarding trademarks. As the courts say, the use cannot be sporadic, casual, and nominal. The use must be active and public. Furthermore, courts frown on creating a "trademark maintenance program" in order to hoard brands or keep competitors from using a mark. Thus, a legitimate business reason for using the brand must exist other than simply trademark maintenance.

Although small quantities of product sales under the brand will not necessarily doom a trademark, courts will consider the amount of sales in determining whether the use of the mark is active and public. The brand owner must demonstrate that it has an active program in which it is attempting to sell the public products under the mark.

Brand owners should keep historical records of brand use that contain at least the following:

- the history of mark selection and approval (who selected and approved the mark and the evolution of the mark during the process);
- the product(s) covered by the mark;
- the marketing and distribution plan for the product(s) under the mark;
- invoices, shipping documents, and publications showing the first use of the mark in state and interstate commerce;
- documents that show the mark as it appeared on product(s) both before and after registration;
- the trademark application and supporting documents for each country in which the mark is registered;
- all correspondence concerning the mark, particularly letters regarding misuse and infringement;
- trademark use manuals related to the mark;
- decrees, orders, and judgments affecting the mark;
- advertising specimen showing continuous advertising under the mark;
- sales and advertising revenue and expenses related to the mark.

These records will be useful in overcoming challenges to the brand by competitors, preparing for infringement litigation regarding the brand, and keeping track of changes in the brand.

To prevent inadvertent abandonment of marks, companies should set up programs of strategic abandonment. Under these programs, companies can seek to capitalize on tax advantages created by affirmatively abandoning trademarks that the company no longer wants to use. Companies can also endeavor to sell the trademark to another. Both these activities can generate revenue for the company and have the added advantage of forcing a business decision on whether to keep using the brand. A form for the sale of a trademark follows.

## TRADEMARK ASSIGNMENT

Assignor, [name of company, state of organization, and place of business], owns the Mark(s) attached as Exhibit A (the "Mark(s)"). Assignee, [name of company, state of organization, and place of business], desires to acquire the Mark(s). For good and valuable consideration of [insert amount], the receipt of which is acknowledged, Assignor assigns to Assignee all rights, title, and interest in the Mark(s), together with the goodwill of the business symbolized by the Mark(s) and any & all registrations of the Mark(s).

[Name of company], Assignee

_____

Name and title

Subscribed and sworn to before me [date].

_____

Notary Public

**Tips on maintaining brands:**

1. Make affirmative decisions whether to keep or abandon a brand. Never inadvertently let brands fall into disuse.

2. Do not create "trademark maintenance programs" designed to keep brands alive for purposes of blocking competition.

3. Find legitimate uses for brands that trade off the brand's good will. Such uses include licensing programs, co-branding, and tribute programs.

4. Keep records of brand use and significant events related to the brand.

5. Attempt to sell, license, or affirmatively abandon brands you no longer intend to use.

# Keeping the Mark Out of the Public Domain

Advertisers often say "Make this brand a household name! When people want widgets, I want them to ask for *Acmes.*" Achieving this goal would represent an expenditure of significant resources and creative genius and would ultimately be rewarded with the loss of the brand. Unbelievably, any brand that achieves advertising's ultimate goal is doomed because the public sees the brand as representing the name of the product rather than the source of the product.

A brand owner must take steps to prevent the public from appropriating the brand as its own. Following the trademark use rules is the best way to protect the brand from public appropriation. This is because the brand owner, as the promoter of the brand, is in the best (and sometimes the only) position to properly educate the public about the brand. Thus, the brand owner should adhere to the following rules in preparing text regarding the brand:

- Always use the mark as an adjective. Never make the mark plural or possessive (plurals and possessives are nouns, not adjectives).

- Never use the mark as a verb.

- Always distinguish the mark from the remaining text.

- Always indicate at least once on each piece of printed material that the brand has trademark status.

- Do not give the mark a definition, except as a trademark of the company.

Remember, the key question the courts will ask in determining whether a brand has lost trademark status is whether the public sees the brand as a trademark or a product name. Courts will also ask whether the public has any other method of referring to the product. Following the rules above will help the public remember that the brand is a trademark rather than a product name.

Also remember that the adjective rule applies only when using the mark in a sentence. A sign or label with just the mark on it does not use the mark as a noun, a verb, or an adjective. It uses the mark as a mark.

A recent advertisement from the *Fulton Daily News* underscores proper and improper trademark care techniques. The advertisement appeared under the headline "A Brand New Wiper That's Already a Household Name."

> Upon hearing the word Teflon®, one might think of non-stick pots and pans, stain repellant carpeting, or even water resistant fabrics. Some may even know that Teflon has recently been used for permanent architectural structures including the Pontiac Silverdome in Detroit, and the Orange Bowl at Syracuse University. But whatever image is conjured in the mind of the consumer, most will agree that the name Teflon itself is synonymous with the features of wearability and durability. Discovered somewhat by accident by a DuPont chemist in 1938, Teflon revolutionized the plastics industry and has since become a household name.

The advertisement goes on to announce the "exclusive introduction of Teflon into" a line of windshield wiper blades. The advertisement does associate "Teflon" with the circled "R" denoting a registered trademark, but otherwise ignores the rules of trademark use. It calls "Teflon" a "word," a "name," and "a household name" instead of a "brand" or a "trademark." It uses "Teflon" repeatedly as a noun instead of an adjective. It gives the brand synonyms, just like an ordinary word. It never once mentions the actual product name, which is polymerized tetrafluoroethylene (TFE). How many people reading the advertisement even know the actual product name? How many think the product name is simply "Teflon"? What impression does this advertisement give, particularly when it goes on to state that a DuPont chemist discovered "Teflon," rather than stating that a DuPont chemist discovered TFE? A corrected version of the advertisement appears below.

> Upon ~~hearing~~ seeing the ~~word~~ Teflon® <u>trademark</u>, one might think of non-stick pots and pans, stain repellant carpeting, or even water resistant fabrics. Some may even know

that Teflon <u>brand polymerized tetrafluoroethylene (TFE)</u> has recently been used for permanent architectural structures including the Pontiac Silverdome in Detroit, and the Orange Bowl at Syracuse University. But whatever image is conjured in the mind of the consumer, most will agree that the ~~name~~ Teflon <u>brand</u> itself ~~is synonymous with the features of~~ <u>represents</u> wearability and durability. Discovered somewhat by accident by a DuPont chemist in 1938, ~~Teflon~~ <u>TFE</u> revolutionized the plastics industry ~~and has since become a household name~~. <u>The "Teflon" mark has come to represent the most recognized brand of TFE.</u>

To DuPont's credit, in 1975 it survived a challenge to "Teflon's" trademark status by producing survey evidence showing that 68 percent of 1,031 respondents on June 4, 1973, thought of "Teflon" as a trademark rather than a common name. *E.I. Du Pont de Nemours & Co. v. Yoshida International, Inc.*, 393 F. Supp. 502 (E.D.N.Y. 1975). But that survey would be of little relevance today, and DuPont's trademark counsel more than likely took steps to make sure such an advertisement will not appear again.

On a recent visit to my pets' veterinarian, I noticed a poster imploring me to "Get the fastest relief. Only Advantage® stops fleas from biting in less than five minutes." In the bottom right corner, I saw a tiny "Advantage" logo, followed by even smaller print stating "(imidacloprid) Topical Solution." In the bottom left corner, I found the advertisement's creator, the Bayer Corporation, the losing author of the famous (in legal circles anyway) 1921 Learned Hand opinion rendering "Aspirin" a generic term, in part because Bayer itself "used the word 'Aspirin' as though it was a general term." *Bayer Co. v. United Drug Co.*, 272 F. 505 (S.D.N.Y. 1921) (L. Hand, J.). While I understood at the time that "Advantage" was a trademark of some company, I was surprised to see that Bayer of all companies was willing to use its brand as a noun, notwithstanding the fine print showing proper usage.

Likewise, Peter Eio, former president of Lego Systems Incorporated, inexplicably wrote a letter to *BusinessWeek* bragging that "LEGO appears in the Concise Oxford English Dictionary."

Finding a mark in a dictionary is one of the first steps to losing it, however, because courts will not protect marks that have become part of everyday speech. "And the dictionary, with its continuing catalogue of words arriving in and departing from common speech, is an especially appropriate source of evidence" that a brand no longer deserves trademark protection. *Gimix, Inc. v. JS&A Group*, 699 F.2d 901, 905 (7th Cir. 1983).

In contrast, both Xerox Corporation (with a brand valued at $5.31 billion by the Interbrand 2002 survey) and Rollerblade Incorporated have released advertisements instructing the public on the proper use of their trademarks. For example, Rollerblade warns consumers that "Because Rollerblade® is a brand name, references to 'rollerblades, rollerbladers, rollerblading, blades, bladers and blading' are incorrect. Proper generic terms for the product, athletes and sport are in-line skates, in-line skaters and in-line skating."

Such advertisements are generally not necessary except in cases where the public might begin adopting the trademark as its own, for example, using the term "xerox" instead of "copy" or the term "rollerblading" instead of "in-line skating." To ensure that the public uses the trademark properly, brand owners should hire a watch service to monitor brand usage in the media. The watch service can also provide information on product reviews, consumer criticism, and other issues important to brand image. While hiring a watch service is relatively inexpensive, it amazes me that companies will hire twenty-four-hour security guards for their tangible assets, yet skimp on a watch service to protect the brand. The watch service essentially acts as a security system for the brand.

When a brand owner finds evidence of misuse in the media, a polite letter requesting proper future use can help correct problems. An example of such a letter follows:

### TRADEMARK MEDIA LETTER

Dear [Editor]:

Re: [name and date of article]

We read the above article with interest and generally enjoy your publication. Unfortunately, the article referred to one of our trademarks as though it were the generic name for all products of that kind. In fact, [trademark] is our company's trademark for [product]. As you probably know, trademarks must always be used as proper adjectives, not as nouns. As the trademark owner, we want to do our best to make sure the media uses our mark properly.

We believe that you strive for accuracy in reporting, so we have enclosed a list of our company trademarks for your editorial staff. If any member of your staff has a question about the proper use of our trademarks or our products, please do not hesitate to call. Thank you for your consideration of this matter.

Sincerely,

---

Just because a mark owner finds his brand in the dictionary or misused by the media does not mean that the mark is forever lost. At one point, several commentators declared the brands "Kleenex" and "Xerox" dead. The owners of these brands, however, waged long-term campaigns to save these marks and educate the public as to their proper use, and many commentators now believe that these efforts have proven successful.

The Singer Manufacturing Company mounted perhaps the most impressive effort in history to reclaim a generic word as a mark through a campaign to resurrect the mark "Singer." In 1896, the United States Supreme Court found that "singer" had passed into the public domain as a generic term for "sewing machine." *Singer Manufacturing Co. v. June Manufacturing Co.*, 163 U.S. 169 (1896). Despite this finding, Singer Manufacturing consistently and persistently used the name "Singer" in designating both sewing machines and other goods manufactured by it. It also advertised the "Singer" name continuously and widely. Finally, more than fifty years later, a court declared that Singer Manufacturing had "recaptured from the public domain the name 'Singer' and...the mark 'Singer'... has thus become a valid trade-mark...and is entitled to protection as such." *Singer Manufacturing Co. v. Briley*, 207 F.2d 519 (5th Cir. 1953).

Singer Manufacturing was helped in its efforts by the failure of its competitors and the media to use "Singer" as a generic word, allowing Singer Manufacturing to have exclusive use of the term during much of the fifty-year quest to regain trademark status. Had the use not been exclusive, the revival effort probably would have failed. Indeed, in 1981 a court observed that by the year of the "Singer" revival, "singer" no longer meant "sewing machine." The court added that where a "term has become obsolete and is discoverable only by resort to historical sources . . . compiled to preserve from oblivion obsolete words, then . . . the word . . . is no longer a generic word." *Miller Brewing Co. v. Falstaff Brewing Corp.*, 655 F.2d 5 (1st Cir. 1981). Thus, even the most heroic and persistent effort cannot revive a brand that the public insists on appropriating as its own.

**Tips on avoiding public appropriation of the brand:**

1.  Follow the trademark use rules. Use the brand in text as an adjective, distinguish the brand from other text, and notify the public that the brand is a trademark.

2.  Strive to associate the brand with your company and not as a generic name for the product. Use the product name along with the brand to educate the public that the brand is not a generic name for the product.

3.  Do not strive to have the brand included in the dictionary or give the brand a definition. If a dictionary lists your brand, then do not celebrate. Ask the dictionary to remove the definition or at least to include a statement that the word is a trademark of the company.

# Avoiding Split Personalities: Not Everything is a Brand

After learning about trademarks, many people go from not caring to the opposite extreme: treating everything as a trademark. This can actually be as dangerous as ignorance. The main traps for the recently enlightened are: (1) going crazy with the Rs and applying trademark registration symbols indiscriminately, which can void marks that are not registered; and (2) branding everything, so that no product names exist and the brand becomes doomed from the start.

In going crazy with the Rs, distinguishing company names from company trademarks generally creates the most confusion. A company name is not a trademark! A company name is just that, the name of the company. Very often, a trademark will make up part of a company name. For example, American Airlines, Inc. is the name of the company that flies airplanes under the "AmericanAirlines" mark. Xerox Corporation is the name of the company that markets documentation products under the "Xerox" mark. And Bank of America Corporation is the name of the company that markets financial services under the "Bank of America" mark. These company names and brands are treated no differently by trademark law than Philip Morris Incorporated, which markets cigarettes under the "Marlboro" mark and cheese under the "Kraft" mark. Just because the mark is part of the company name does not mean that the company name is a trademark. In fact, it is just the opposite: The corporate name is almost never a trademark. Thus, the following are incorrect uses of the company name and the trademark registration symbol:

- Xerox Corporation®;
- Xerox® Corporation;
- Xerox® announced today that its quarterly profits will exceed Wall Street expectations.

This is probably one of the most difficult concepts in branding. Even the so-called experts who claim to understand trademarks and branding get it wrong. Alex Frankel, who wrote *3-2-1 Launch!*, a book about brand names and their impact on language published by John Wiley & Sons, noted in a September 2, 2001, *New York Times* magazine article that lawyers "prefer that the trademark not be used as a verb. The legal guns at Xerox® and Hoover® feel the same way about *xeroxing* and *hoovering*."

The quoted use of "Xerox® and Hoover®" violates two rules of trademark law: (1) Always use the mark as an adjective; and (2) Do not confuse the mark with the company name. The article's author could have easily corrected the sentence by removing the "®" next to "Xerox and Hoover", as he is using the words as corporate names, not trademarks.

Company names are not trademarks. Indeed, the United States Patent and Trademark Office generally will not register a company name as a trademark. In fact, uses like those cited above basically tell the world, "Hey, this is our trademark, and we're using it as a noun!" It is actually better *not* to have the registration symbol in printed material than to misuse it.

The example above demonstrates the main area where people misunderstand the difference between corporate names and brands. Using the short form of a corporate name (Xerox as short for Xerox Corporation) does *not* convert the corporate name into a brand. For example, Ralph Lauren the fashion designer has a "Ralph Lauren" brand clothing line through his company, Polo Ralph Lauren Corporation. Just because the name "Ralph Lauren" is a brand does not mean that a registration mark must appear by Ralph Lauren when referring to the person. Thus, the proper use of the registration mark would be as follows:

> Designer Ralph Lauren will unveil his new line of Ralph Lauren® clothing at a fashion show tomorrow.

The first reference in the sentence is to Ralph Lauren the person. The name is properly used as a noun. The second reference is to "Ralph Lauren" brand clothing. Here, the "Ralph Lauren" trademark is properly used as an adjective.

Likewise, corporate names are used the same way:

Xerox will unveil its new line of Xerox® copiers at a trade show tomorrow.

The first reference in the sentence is to Xerox Corporation, which is properly used as a noun. The second reference is to "Xerox" brand copiers, which is properly used as an adjective.

When questions arise, the best way to distinguish these two uses is to mentally insert the words "brand" and "corporation" into the sentence. When "Corporation" (or "Company," "Incorporated," etc.) logically follows, do not use the trademark designation. When "brand" logically follows, use the trademark designation.

*CORRECT*:

Xerox [Corporation] will unveil its new line of Xerox® [brand] copiers at a trade show tomorrow.

*INCORRECT*:

Xerox® [brand] will unveil its new line of Xerox [Corporation] copiers at a trade show tomorrow.

In addition, companies must separate the corporate trademark from the corporate name. Thus, business cards and letterhead using the brand should not have the business address near the brand. Examples of correct and incorrect letterhead and business cards follow.

**CORRECT LETTERHEAD**

**ACME®**

1234 Main Street, Dallas, Texas 75201

## INCORRECT LETTERHEAD

# ACME®

1234 Main Street, Dallas, Texas 75201

## CORRECT LETTERHEAD

**Acme, Inc.**

1234 Main Street, Dallas, Texas 75201

## CORRECT BUSINESS CARDS

| **Acme, Inc.**<br><br>1234 Main Street<br>Dallas, Texas 75206<br><br>Bill Johnson<br>President | **ACME®**<br><br>Bill Johnson<br>President<br><br>1234 Main Street<br>Dallas, Texas 75201 |
|---|---|

## INCORRECT BUSINESS CARDS

| | |
|---|---|
| **ACME**® <br><br> 1234 Main Street <br> Dallas, Texas 75201 <br><br> Bill Johnson <br> President | Bill Johnson <br> President <br><br> **ACME**® <br> 1234 Main Street <br> Dallas, Texas 75201 |

The key element on the incorrect stationary and business cards is that the mark appears next to the address, making the mark look like the company name. The correct stationary and business card samples either separate the mark from the address or use the company name instead of the mark when the two appear next to each other. The rule should be the same for envelopes. If an envelope contains the company mark, separate the return address by either placing it on the other side of the envelope or some other place distinct from the mark. If you absolutely must place the address near the mark, then use the company name as part of the address to make the proper distinction. For example:

**ACME**®

Acme, Inc.

1234 Main Street

Dallas, Texas 75201

The second common problem for the newly enlightened is the effort to brand everything, applying ™s to every word in the corporate lexicon. Unfortunately, it is not that simple. In fact, overuse of the ™ symbol has caused some courts to look skeptically upon all of a company's trademarks, legitimate or not.

The basic question to ask with every brand is "what's your noun?" The brand must be an adjective, which means it must attach to a noun. This is most likely to happen with new products or chemically based products like drugs that have complicated names. (The generic name for aspirin was acetylsalicylic acid. How many consumers remembered that?)

Incorporating nouns into trademarks also occurs with common products, however, even with products marketed by people who should know better. For example, Godwin Gruber, which has a reputation as an excellent law firm, has trademarked "Mission Critical Litigation." When used in a sentence, however, Godwin Gruber constantly uses it as a noun. For example, "Godwin Gruber's experience in Mission Critical Litigation™ is the foundation for maximum effective enforcement of client patents, trademarks or copyrights."

What choice does the firm have? Any other use would be redundant ("Mission Critical Litigation™ litigation") or awkward (Mission Critical Litigation™ legal services"). A much better trademark would be "Mission Critical"™, which the firm could attach to various nouns describing legal services. In fact, Godwin Gruber at various sections of its Web site attaches "Mission Critical" to other nouns, reporting that "There is no more Mission Critical area of legal practice than health law" and "There is no more Mission Critical task for any business than to raise the capital necessary for operations and growth. . . ."

A similar problem arises for companies marketing recently invented products. These companies often discover that an overly descriptive trademark can become a household name and eclipse the product name to the point where the mark becomes generic. Sailboard manufacturer Windsurfer International Incorporated, for example, lost its marks "Windsurfer," "Windsurfing," and "Wind Surf" due to generic use. *Windsurfer International Inc. v. Fred Ostermann, GmbH*, 613 F. Supp. 933 (S.D.N.Y. 1985), *vacated*, 828 F.2d 755 (Fed. Cir. 1987). The decision was overturned on a technicality: lack of jurisdiction because the court found that the plaintiff was seeking an advisory opinion as to whether it could use the mark. To avoid the fate Windsurfer International nearly averted, in-line skate manufacturer Rollerblade Incorporated has begun advertising to prevent customers from calling in-line skates "rollerblades."

Even nondescriptive marks can become generic if promoted without regard to the true name of the product. Donald F. Duncan Incorporated used its "Yo-Yo" brand with wild abandon until struck with the realization that no one knew that the generic name for its product was a return top. Duncan recognized the problem it had created too late to remove the word from common speech.

With the increasing use of the Internet, companies have started using two relatively new branding items: meta-tags and domain names. The United States Patent and Trademark Office has gotten increasingly strict on granting trademark status to domain names, treating them like addresses. To get trademark status, the domain name must stand for something more than simply a web address where customers can buy products available elsewhere.

On its Web site, the USPTO sets out its criteria for granting trademark registration to certain domain names. Generally, the mark must be used as more than an Internet address and must stand for something other than simply advertising the domain holder's goods and services.

> If the proposed mark is used in a way that would be perceived as nothing more than an Internet address where the applicant can be contacted, registration must be refused. Examples of a domain name used only as an Internet address include a domain name used in close proximity to language referring to the domain name as an address, or a domain name displayed merely as part of the information on how to contact the applicant.

>> *Example*: The mark is WWW.ABC.COM for on-line ordering services in the field of clothing. Specimens of use consisting of an advertisement that states "visit us on the web at www.ABC.com" do not show service mark use of the proposed mark.

*Example*: The mark is ABC.COM for financial consulting services. Specimens of use consisting of a business card that refers to the service and lists a phone number, fax number, and the domain name sought to be registered do not show service mark use of the proposed mark.

If the specimens of use fail to show the domain name used as a mark and the applicant seeks registration on the Principal Register, the examining attorney must refuse registration on the ground that the matter presented for registration does not function as a mark. [...]

Advertising one's own products or services is not a service. Therefore, businesses that create a web site for the sole purpose of advertising their own products or services cannot register a domain name used to identify that activity. In examination, the issue usually arises when the applicant describes the activity as a registrable service, *e.g.*, "providing information about [a particular field]," but the specimens of use make it clear that the web site merely advertises the applicant's own products or services. In this situation, the examining attorney must refuse registration because the mark is used to identify an activity that does not constitute a "service" within the meaning of the Trademark Act.

Meta tags are used by search engines to lead customers to appropriate Web sites. Meta tags are essentially a list of words and phrases that the Web site owner believes are appropriate to directing a Web surfer to the site. These words and phrases consist of generic terms and trademarks as well. For example, Ford Motor Company might use generic meta tags such as car, automobile, driving, pickup, convertible, 4x4, and wheels, and trademark meta tags such as "Ford," "Mustang," "F-150," and "Explorer." Could Ford also use the meta tags "Chevrolet" and "Dodge"? If someone does a web search for "Dodge Ram pickups," do they want to be directed to Ford's Web site? Some courts have found that including a competitor's trademark in a list of meta tags constitutes unfair competition.

Specifically, one court found that including the trademarked term "MovieBuff" in meta tags would result in what it called "initial interest confusion" among consumers. *Brookfield Communications, Inc. v. West Coast Entertainment Corp.*, 174 F.3d 1036 (9th Cir. 1999). The court reasoned that, while meta tags are hidden from consumer view and thus not likely to themselves cause confusion, the redirecting of Internet traffic to a Web site through using another's trademark would divert consumers from the trademarked Web site:

> Although entering "MovieBuff" into a search engine is likely to bring up a list including "westcoastvideo.com" if West Coast has included that term in its meta tags, the resulting confusion is not as great as where West Coast uses the "moviebuff.com" domain name. First, when the user inputs "MovieBuff" into an Internet search engine, the list produced by the search engine is likely to include both West Coast's and Brookfield's web sites. Thus, in scanning such a list, the Web user will often be able to find the particular web site he is seeking. Moreover, even if the Web user chooses the web site belonging to West Coast, he will see that the domain name of the web site he selected is "westcoastvideo.com." Since there is no confusion resulting from the domain address, and since West Coast's initial web page prominently displays its own name, it is difficult to say that a consumer is likely to be confused about whose site he has reached or to think that Brookfield somehow sponsors West Coast's web site.
>
> Nevertheless, West Coast's use of "moviebuff.com" in meta tags will still result in what is known as initial interest confusion. Web surfers looking for Brookfield's "MovieBuff" products who are taken by a search engine to "westcoastvideo.com" will find a database similar enough to "MovieBuff" such that a sizeable number of consumers who were originally looking for Brookfield's product will simply decide to utilize West Coast's offerings instead. Although

there is no source confusion in the sense that consumers know they are patronizing West Coast rather than Brookfield, there is nevertheless initial interest confusion in the sense that, by using "moviebuff.com" or "MovieBuff" to divert people looking for "MovieBuff" to its web site, West Coast improperly benefits from the goodwill that Brookfield developed in its mark.

In rendering this decision, the court analogized the meta tag to a deceptive road sign:

> Using another's trademark in one's meta tags is much like posting a sign with another's trademark in front of one's store. Suppose West Coast's, [the defendant's], competitor (let's call it "Blockbuster") puts up a billboard on a highway reading—"West Coast Video: 2 miles ahead at Exit 7"— where West Coast is really located at Exit 8 but Blockbuster is located at Exit 7. Customers looking for West Coast's store will pull off at Exit 7 and drive around looking for it. Unable to locate West Coast, but seeing the Blockbuster store right by the highway entrance, they may simply rent there. Even consumers who prefer West Coast may find it not worth the trouble to continue searching for West Coast since there is a Blockbuster right there.

Of course, a search engine generates numerous directions to sites, not just one, and it is far easier to click back to the search engine and pick the correct site than to reenter the highway and find a store through a maze of streets. However, the analogy still demonstrates that companies must be careful in using other's marks, even in Web site text. Indeed, a recent district court order took the *Brookfield Communications* decision even further, enjoining a Web site from using a competitor's trade name in text more than was "reasonably necessary to identify the competitor's services," which included prohibitions on placing the trade name in larger or more prominent text and on using header and underline tags around sentences including the name. *J.K. Harris & Co. v. Kassel*, 62 U.S.P.Q.2d 1926 (N.D. Cal. 2002).

## Tips on avoiding overbranding

1. Do not apply the trademark or registration symbol to every word in the corporate vocabulary. Some things are not brands.

2. Make sure every brand also has a generic product name.

3. Ask the question "What's the noun?" when creating a brand.

4. Keep the brand name distinct from the company name. Using the short form of the company name (Xerox for Xerox Corporation) does not convert the company name into a brand, even if the short form of the company name *is* a brand when used as an adjective ("Xerox" brand copiers).

5. Avoid placing the brand near the corporate address on stationary, business cards, envelopes, signs, and advertisements.

6. You cannot trademark a domain name unless the domain name also functions as an identifier of a source of goods or services. It cannot simply function as a Web address, and the Web site must be more than an advertisement for the owner's products.

7. Companies that use competitors' trademarks as meta tags could be at risk for unfair competition lawsuits.

# Putting It in Writing: Protecting Your Brand in Contracts

When a trademark is sold, the agreement evidencing the sale must be in writing. When a trademark is licensed for use by another, the agreement need not be in writing. Likewise, permission to use a trademark also need not be in writing. Given the value of a brand, however, every license and permitted use should be in writing. In fact, this should be a company policy.

For example, Hertz will not allow a customer to rent a $20,000 car without first executing a multipage agreement covering everything from age restrictions to the guaranteed rate period. Should Hertz be any less protective of its brand, which the 2002 Interbrand survey valued at $3.36 billion? Granting a naked license to use the brand constitutes abandonment of the brand. In other words, a brand owner that allows another to sell products under the brand without exercising control of the quality of those products loses the brand.

Even without this legal requirement, it makes business sense for a brand owner to exercise control over the way its brand is used by others. For example, in 1997 American Airlines placed the "AmericanAirlines" brand in the movie *Jungle 2 Jungle*, only to watch one of the actors urinate in the aisle of the airplane—not exactly the message one hopes to send through product placement. Worse, the movie *Charlie's Angels* features an actress holding up one of Microsoft's "Pocket PC" handhelds and exclaiming "Palm Pilot!"

A brand owner who wishes to allow another to use its mark has two options: (1) enter a license agreement and monitor the use of the mark; or (2) consent to the use and in effect concede that the use does not infringe on the mark. This is a difficult and serious choice. Under the license agreement, the brand owner must monitor the use or face the possibility of issuing a naked license, which can result in loss of the mark. Under the consent to use, the brand owner effectively admits that the use does not infringe on the mark, and therefore the brand owner cannot control its use. Some courts have actually held that a consent to use in one instance precludes infringement actions for all uses of the mark of that type.

## The License Agreement

Whenever a brand owner wants to allow another party to use the brand in a way that could confuse consumers into believing that the other party is associated with the brand, the brand owner must issue a license to use the brand. With a license agreement, the brand owner retains ownership of the brand, but allows another to use it in a controlled manner. *The essential part of any license agreement is that the brand owner actually monitors and controls the quality of the products that the licensee produces under the brand.* A license agreement should establish the brand owner's right to exercise this control. A sample barebones license agreement containing the basic provisions follows.

### TRADEMARK LICENSE AGREEMENT

Licensor, [name of company, state of organization, and place of business], owns the Mark(s) attached as Exhibit A. Licensor agrees to grant Licensee, [name of company and place of business], an [exclusive/nonexclusive] license to use the Mark(s) only in the manner set forth in Exhibit B. Licensee agrees it will pay Licensor the amounts set forth in the schedule attached as Exhibit C.

The parties expressly agree that Licensor retains full ownership of the Mark(s) and any application or registration of the Mark(s). Licensee agrees it will do nothing inconsistent with Licensor's ownership, application, or registration of the Mark(s), and Licensee will not use any word(s) or symbol(s) in a manner that is confusingly similar to Licensor's use of the Mark(s). Licensee further agrees not to attack Licensor's title in the Mark(s) or the validity of this License. Licensee's use of the Mark(s) shall inure to the benefit of and be on behalf of Licensor. Licensee understands that nothing in this License shall give Licensee any right, title, or interest in the Mark(s), except the right to use the Mark(s) in accordance with this License.

Licensee shall maintain the quality of all goods and services sold under the Mark(s) in accordance with the specifications set forth in Exhibit D, as amended by Licensor from time to time. The parties agree Licensor retains the right to inspect the quality of goods or services sold under the Mark(s) to ensure Licensee meets Licensor's specifications. Licensee agrees to maintain books and records relating to its activities set forth in Exhibit B, which Licensee shall make available for inspection upon Licensor's request during normal business hours.

This License shall be effective beginning [date]. Licensee may not assign this License without Licensor's prior written consent.

Either party may terminate this License on [number] days' notice. Upon termination of this License, Licensee shall immediately (1) cease all use of the Mark(s); (2) cease all use of any word(s) or symbol(s) used in a manner confusingly similar to Licensor's use of the Mark(s); and (3) destroy all material containing the Mark(s). Licensee agrees that upon termination of this License all right, title, and interest in the Mark(s) and the good will connected to the Mark(s) remains Licensor's property.

AGREED:                           AGREED:

_____          _____


This agreement, though bare bones, is weighted toward protecting the brand owner. For example, under this agreement, the brand owner can terminate the agreement at any time, for any reason, and require the licensee to immediately destroy all material containing the brand. Theoretically, the brand owner without notice could destroy the licensee's entire inventory. This would most likely be unacceptable to the licensee, who would want to negotiate a notice period and some provision for disposing of the material containing the brand upon termination.

In addition, most license agreements would be much longer than the sample given here. Even this simplified license requires additional provisions in the form of Exhibits A to D. Exhibit A should contain either a description, the registration number, or a picture of the mark(s). I prefer attaching a picture and the registration number (if any) of any mark under license. This avoids confusion.

Exhibit B should also be as specific as possible. It should state the exact circumstances under which the licensee can use the mark(s), and which products the licensee can attach to the mark(s). It should also provide a list of trade names, trademarks, service marks, and trade dress that the licensee can associate with the mark(s), and should prohibit the licensee from using the mark(s) in conjunction with any other trade name, trade dress, trademark, or service mark without first obtaining the brand owner's express written consent.

Exhibit C can contain whatever payment terms the parties negotiate, including up-front fees, royalties, or both. This will vary widely depending on the circumstances.

Exhibit D should set forth both the brand owner's specific trademark standards and the inspection requirements. It can be as simple as stating that "Licensee shall abide by Licensor's quality standards with respect to the Mark(s)." I would recommend, however, that this provision at least include requirements that:

- licensee shall abide by licensor's brand standards manual;

- licensee shall abide by licensor's quality standards manual;

- licensee shall provide licensor with a sample of all products and materials bearing the mark(s);

- licensee shall obtain the mark(s) from a single source, such as a restricted-access Web site containing downloadable graphics or an individual responsible for the mark(s).

Trademark licensors and licensees should also consider adding to the license agreement requirements that:

- define the territory in which the licensee may use the mark(s);

- the licensee use its "best efforts" in marketing products under the mark(s);

- the licensee assist the licensor as necessary in obtaining or maintaining any registration of the mark(s);

- The licensee notify the mark owner upon threat or receipt of litigation involving the mark(s);

- The licensor preapprove all material containing the mark(s);

- permit or prevent the sublicensing of the licensee's rights;

- prevent the license from creating an agency relationship or joint venture between the parties;

- state that the license constitutes the entire agreement between the parties with respect to the mark(s) and may be modified only by a signed writing;

- guarantee that the licensor is sole owner of the mark(s);

- provide minimum or maximum sales requirements;

- give the licensee access to the licensor's "internal markets" in selling the licensed products;

- indemnify the licensor for liability involving products produced under the mark(s);

- indemnify the licensee for liability involving use of the mark(s);

- provide minimum insurance sufficient to satisfy the indemnification requirements;

- obligate the licensee to assist in preventing trademark infringement by third parties;

- prevent the licensee from marketing competitive products;

- establish governing law and jurisdiction in the event of a dispute;

- enforce mediation and/or binding arbitration in the event of a dispute;

- automatically terminate the license on a set date or event (such as bankruptcy or insolvency);

- provide conditions for termination (such as "for cause");
- provide for disposing of materials bearing the mark(s) on termination.

If a brand owner wishes to convert an oral license into a written license, the brand owner can do so with a clause stating that the new written license relates back to the date the oral license was entered. Courts will generally uphold these contracts if the written agreement accurately reflects the oral agreement.

### The Consent to Use

At times, a brand owner may want to allow another party to use the brand in a way that is not likely to cause confusion as to the source of the product containing the brand. For example, in Dallas, Texas, local sculptors displayed around town their interpretations of Mobil's Pegasus symbol. By allowing this use to take place, Mobil in effect admitted that the public would not be led to believe that Mobil was the source of the winged horse sculptures. Mobil also had the option of committing to writing its agreement that the particular sculptures did not constitute a trademark infringement through a consent-to-use agreement.

The consent to use erodes trademark rights, however, because it is an admission that a certain use does not infringe on the mark owner's rights. This admission exempts a category of use from trademark enforcement. Furthermore, that exempted category can open a floodgate of other unanticipated exempted uses.

For example, this book quotes a court making the slam dunk conclusion that "[w]e think it plain that the likelihood of confusion and mistake is present" between "Black & White" whiskey and "Black & White" beer. A consent to use agreement, however, can turn a slam-dunk infringement into a noninfringement. For example, the owner of "Skol" vodka consented that a beer company could register "Skol" beer. When "Skol" beer opposed Canada Dry's registration of "Skola" cola, the court found that the beer and vodka maker's mutual agreement that "Skol" beer and "Skol" vodka could coexist without likely confusion supported the conclusion that "Skol" beer and "Skola" cola could coexist without likely confusion. *Swedish Beer Export Co. v. Canada Dry Corp.*, 469 F.2d 1096 (C.C.P.A. 1972).

Because consenting to use is an admission that public confusion about the use of the mark is unlikely, a brand owner does not need to monitor and control the permitted use. However, issuing a license under the guise of a consent to use does not exempt a brand owner from the monitoring and control requirement. In fact, this would be the worst of all worlds because a competitor could argue that the brand owner either admitted non-infringement or issued a naked license. The brand winds up bleeding no matter which side of the blade cuts.

## PERMITTED USE LICENSE
### (Requires monitoring by the mark owner)

This letter grants you permission to affix the attached trademarks, service marks, and/or copyrighted material (the "Marks") in connection with your business of [description] and for the following purposes only: [use] (the "Permitted Use"). You understand and acknowledge that [Brand Owner] owns the Marks and that you have no right to alienate the Marks. You further understand that you have no right or permission to use any other Marks owned by [Brand Owner] or its affiliated entities, nor do you have permission to use the Marks for any purpose not expressly stated above.

[Brand Owner] will provide you samples of the Marks that conform to [Brand Owner's] corporate graphics standards. Under no circumstances will you (1) use or display any [Brand Owner] Marks that you have not obtained from [Brand Owner]; (2) alter the Marks in any way; or (3) display the Marks without the appropriate proprietary rights notices.

You agree that you will provide [Brand Owner] samples of your use of the mark before disseminating any products or material containing the mark to its intended audience. Your provision of materials to [Brand Owner] that do not conform to the Permitted Use do not constitute a modification of the Permitted Use or a waiver of [Brand Owner's] rights in the Marks or under this letter, even if [Brand Owner] does not object to the materials before you disseminate the materials to the public.

You agree that [Brand Owner] can, at any time and at its sole discretion, retract this permission to use the Marks. [Brand Owner] can make this decision without warning, for a good reason, a bad reason, or no reason at all. You agree that upon receiving written notice that [Brand Owner] has revoked this permission to use, you will immediately cease and desist using the Marks in any form, including refraining from distributing any previously printed material bearing the Marks. You further agree that you will not use any trademarks or service marks confusingly similar to the Marks.

You understand that you have no rights in the Marks, nor can your continued use of the Marks ever give you any rights in the Marks. Therefore, your use of the Marks (or any demand by [Brand Owner] that you cease using the Marks) can never form the basis of any claim by you for legal relief against [Brand Owner].

Finally, you agree to indemnify, defend and hold harmless [Brand Owner], as well as [Brand Owner's] Affiliates and licensees, and each of their officers, shareholders, directors, employees and agents (collectively, the "[Brand Owner] Indemnified Parties") from and against any and all liabilities, obligations, losses, damages, claims, demands, suits, actions, deficiencies, penalties, taxes, levies, fines, judgments, settlements, costs, expenses, legal fees and disbursements, and accountants' fees and disbursements (collectively, "Losses") incurred by, borne by or asserted against any of the [Brand Owner] Indemnified Parties in any way relating to, arising out of or resulting from your use of the Marks.

If you agree with these terms, please sign below where indicated and return this letter to me no later than [date].

Sincerely,                                    Agreed:

_____          _____

## CONSENT-TO-USE LETTER
### (Does not require monitoring but can exempt a category of uses from enforcement)

This letter consents to your use of [Brand Owner's] trademarks in the manner displayed on the attached [number] sample(s). For this consent to be binding, you must place on the published material the following statement: "Used by permission of [Brand Owner]. [Brand Owner] does not manufacture, sell, or distribute the goods or services advertised herein."

If you agree with these terms, please sign below where indicated and return this letter to me no later than [date].

Sincerely,                                    Agreed:

_____          _____

This consent-to-use letter attempts to limit the scope of the consent by forcing the user to include the statement that "[Brand Owner] does not manufacture, distribute, or sell the goods or services advertised herein." These words help prevent a future infringer from arguing that the consent to use implicitly admitted noninfringement on a category of products because the brand owner can argue that the qualification instead of the type of products offered under the mark prevented confusion.

**The samples above are examples only. I highly recommend using competent legal counsel in negotiating a trademark license and preparing a consent to use, in part because licensing can also subject the licensor to franchise laws and antitrust laws. Antitrust**

laws can carry criminal penalties. *It is not worth saving a few bucks on a lawyer if it lands you in jail.*

**Tips on creating licensing agreements and consents to use:**

1. Monitoring trademark use is the most important part of any license agreement.

2. Converting an oral license agreement to a written license agreement is permissible if the written license agreement reflects the terms of the oral agreement.

3. Consent-to-use agreements help avoid disputes and do not require monitoring. A consent-to-use agreement is an admission that the permitted use does not infringe. Thus, a consent to use may be viewed as evidence that a similar use does not infringe on the mark.

# Watching 'em Like a Hawk: Monitoring Trademark Use

The most important aspect of monitoring trademark use is that *it must be done*. How monitoring is accomplished depends largely on individual circumstances. But the bottom-line question a court will ask in determining whether the monitoring was adequate to prevent a naked license is whether the trademark owner through the monitoring program *actually exercised control over the quality of the products sold under the mark*. If the trademark owner made no such efforts, or inadequate efforts, then the mark is lost.

From a practical perspective, licensors should incorporate some or all of these elements into a licensing program:

- review designs, formulae, ingredients, production requirements, and specifications at an early stage;
- review product samples at least before public sale, if not at each stage in production;
- review samples of advertising, labels, packaging, and other marketing materials before publication;
- periodically review products;
- inspect licensee production facilities;
- inspect some licensee points of sale;
- audit licensee income.

Whether a quality-control program adequately protects the mark is a case-by-case determination and frankly varies from court to court, giving rise to some seemingly inconsistent decisions. In some cases, courts have ignored years of neglect. In other cases, courts have subjected the licensor to increased scrutiny. Thus, even though some courts have refused to find a naked license based on some of the following circumstances, the following monitoring programs have also been found inadequate to ensure the quality of the products sold under the mark:

- relying on the licensee's reputation for excellence;
- absence of complaints involving the quality of licensed products;
- relying on a prior business relationship with the licensee;
- a single inspection of the products produced under the mark.

In addition to a monitoring program, a brand owner should keep a licensing file, which contains at least the following:

- the license agreement;
- correspondence related to the license;
- a quality-control log showing the date, time, place of any inspection or test, the corrective action required if any, and the steps taken to ensure corrective measures;
- samples of labels and advertising.

An inspection program can go too far, however. "Significant control" over the licensee can result in a franchise relationship, which is subject to strict federal and state franchise rules, as well as potential penalties for failure to comply. The Federal Trade Commission offers a complex definition of a "franchise," but part of the definition requires that:

- the franchisor exerts or has authority to exert a significant degree of control over the franchisee's method of operation, including but not limited to, the franchisee's business organization, promotional activities, management, marketing plan, or business affairs; or
- the franchisor gives significant assistance to the franchisee in the latter's method of operation, including, but not limited to, the franchisee's business organization, management, marketing plan, promotional activities, or business affairs; *provided, however,* that assistance in the franchisee's promotional activities shall not, in the absence of assistance in other areas of the franchisee's method of operation, constitute significant assistance; or
- the franchisee offers, sells, or distributes to any person other than

a franchisor, goods, commodities, or services which are:

1. supplied by the franchisor; or

2. supplied by a third person (e.g., a supplier) with whom the franchisee is directly or indirectly required to do business by the franchisor; or

3. supplied by a third person (e.g., a supplier) with whom the franchisee is directly or indirectly advised to do business by the franchisor where such third person is affiliated with the franchisor.

Adding to the complexity, state law may define a franchise differently. And as noted earlier, antitrust laws may also apply to a licensing relationship. In one case, a court found that requiring the purchase of supplies from the licensor constituted an illegal tie-in. *Siegel v. Chicken Delight, Inc.*, 448 F.2d 43 (9th Cir. 1971), *cert. denied*, 405 U.S. 955 (1972). A later case allowed such purchases based on an "inextricable" link between the licensed trademark ("Baskin-Robbins") and the product (ice cream). *Krehl v. Baskin-Robbins Ice Cream Co.*, 664 F.2d 1348 (9th Cir. 1982).

**Tips on monitoring trademark use:**

1. Monitor the quality of products produced under license.

2. Adequate monitoring will vary according to each situation, but the basic element is to ensure that the products under license meet the licensor's quality standards. If you have little notion of what the licensee is doing under the mark, then the mark is in danger.

3. Be careful not to inadvertently create a franchise relationship by exercising significant control over the licensee.

# Slapping Grubby Hands: Trademark Enforcement

Trademark enforcement is a necessary part of brand ownership. While a trademark owner does not need to sniff out and squash every instance of infringement, brand owners must make an effort to prevent infringement and to deal with those instances of infringement that come to their attention.

Sometimes a seemingly innocuous infringement can work to portray the company in a negative light. For example, the July 2001 cover of *Popular Mechanics* magazine featured a "Warp Speed Airliner" called the X-43 painted in the "AmericanAirlines" livery. The accompanying article discussed how the experimental X-43 could fly at Mach-10 and revolutionize commercial air travel. American, however, had nothing to do with the X-43. The real X-43 was black and carried the NASA logo. The article correctly identified NASA as the X-43's sponsor, but the cover and accompanying illustrations gave the impression that American Airlines sponsored the project. Unfortunately, when *Popular Mechanics* created the artwork for the article (without American's permission), it had no way of knowing that right before the issue hit the newsstands, the unmanned X-43 would crash into the Pacific Ocean during a test flight. Thus, a gesture that *Popular Mechanics* thought would bring good will to American by associating American's brand with innovation backfired, instead associating American with a crashing airplane.

The best source of finding infringers is company employees and customers. While a company cannot expect its customers to enforce its brand, it can become aware of infringement through casual conversations with customers or through customer confusion over similar brands. When such instances come to the company's attention, the company should investigate the potential infringement, make a determination whether it is an infringement, and take the appropriate action. While the cheapest and easiest course of action is to do nothing, this is not always the most appropriate course of action. For example, a determination by a company that something does not infringe sets a precedent that may prevent a finding of infringement along similar lines at a later date, particularly when the mark owner enters into a consent agreement with the potential infringer.

Some courts have hinted that this is unfair: The judicial policy is to encourage settlement of disputes, not discourage settlement by allowing later infringers to wield the consent agreement as a shield against the mark owner. Other courts essentially force the mark owner entering into a consent agreement to consent to all uses of that type, even by infringers unknown at the time of the consent agreement. Thus, a mark owner must make a careful determination as to whether a consent agreement will negatively affect its ability to control its mark against future infringement.

Companies can encourage employees to report infringement primarily through education. Companies can also offer token rewards to people who report infringement, such as "logo police" badges or other fun items designed to stimulate conversation about the topic. Employees should understand what constitutes potential infringement and know who to report to when they discover an infringement.

Most trademark infringers are likely to fall into six categories: (1) fans; (2) customers; (3) vendors; (4) potential licensees; (5) employees; (6) critics; and (7) jerks. Other than the final two categories, these other potential infringers are not people that a company wants to offend. Despite this fact, some trademark attorneys have a habit of sending incredibly nasty letters to potential trademark infringers. This is almost always a bad idea as a first point of contact. First, the recipient is often infringing out of ignorance in a misguided attempt to "help" the company. Getting a letter from a lawyer filled with legalese and threatening litigation will not endear this person to the company.

Second, if the infringer is a company critic, then the letter will be used as evidence of the company's heavy-handedness. Frequently, consumer critics will supply the letter to the media or post the letter on a Web site. Third, a company can always ratchet up the rhetoric by following up with a stronger response. It is difficult, however, to retract a harsh letter to someone who thought he was doing the company a favor.

Lawyers get letters from attorneys all the time. The language used in these letters can seem harsh to a nonlawyer while not causing an attorney to bat an eye. When a nonlawyer gets a letter from an attorney, it is often a threatening event. This is why the Coca-Cola Company runs its trademark enforcement letters through the marketing department before sending them. It recognizes that the behavior of every arm of the company business reflects on the company brand. Not surprisingly, the "Coca-Cola" trademark is the world's most valuable brand.

By contrast, Palm Incorporated sent what it believed to be a very polite letter to the owners of Web sites providing support and advice for the use of "Palm" handhelds. Palm wanted to encourage these web sites because they helped fuel demand for the handhelds. Palm worried about the potential abuse of its trademark, however, particularly in the domain names of web sites providing "Palm" handheld support services.

According to a September 19, 2001, article by Ian Fried of CNET News.com, Palm intended the letters to be nonthreatening, beginning one such letter by stating that "Palm Inc. is proud to have a positive relationship with Web sites promoting the Palm OS. We do not in any way want this relationship to deteriorate." But the letter's tone eventually changed: "We must insist that you work with us to re-brand your Web site in a manner that does not infringe Palm's trademark rights." The letter asked for a response within two weeks.

According to Fried, Palmguru.com responded by deciding to change its name to PocketAnywhere.com, and Palmgoddess.com became Pocketgoddess.com. Both name changes reflect the "Pocket PC" product of Palm's rival Microsoft.

Fried reported that Palm began back-pedaling, quoting a Palm representative as saying that Palm was still open to talking to those who received letters. "We hope that people aren't making hasty decisions based on a letter because we did invite them to discuss alternatives. The door is still open."

Fried's quotes of the "Palm" handheld enthusiasts, however, demonstrated some skepticism:

"My new site design is around Pocket PC. Palm is secondary at this point," said Palmguru.com's operator, who said the letter did not sound friendly to him. "I decided it would be best for me to change the name [to PocketAnywhere.com] because I never wanted this issue to rise up again."

"I launched [Palmgoddess.com] on Wednesday," said a longtime "Palm" handheld enthusiast. "And Thursday when I came back from lunch [I had] that letter." She said she decided to change the name to avoid a legal battle.

"We support Palm so much and yet they are hassling us," said another enthusiast who had not yet decided how to respond to Palm's letter.

Palm eventually made peace with some of its enthusiasts, including PalmStation.com, who claimed that Palm had "decided not [to pursue] people [for] having the word 'palm' in their domain names." The names of Palmguru.com and Palmgoddess.com remain changed, although the "palmgoddess.com" address lands one at Pocketgoddess.com. Meanwhile, the former PalmGuru.com site now features a series of articles titled "Crossing Over, Moving from the Palm OS® to Pocket PC."

A lawsuit against Microsoft over the "Palm" trademark likely influenced Palm's decision to send the letters. That suit resulted in a settlement where Microsoft could not use the "Palm" mark, but could refer to a handheld as a "palm-sized PC."

Although most attorneys would not find Palm's trademark enforcement letters particularly threatening, the comments on the Palm enthusiast Web sites demonstrate that nonlawyers view such letters very differently. The reactions were overwhelmingly negative and illustrate typical reactions to infringement letters.

They seem to want to kill off the palmpilot userculture that has been doing their product nothing but good, idiots.

This is one of the stupidest things I have ever seen any company do. . . . I hope this idiocy results in the biggest letter writing campaign in Internet history. . . .

. . . this letter is quite arrogant and hostile. It is not my job to promote 3com's brand. It is not my job to use their trademarks consistently.

this is sheer craziness. how can having the name of a product as your topic be [illegal].

I hate to burst 3com's bubble, but I believe Hewlett Packard has a trademark on "Palmtop."

They need to grow up, get a life and stop telling people what words to use.

Palm's letter was rather lengthy and gave substantial instruction about the proper use of the trademark. It also threatened developers who did not voluntarily remove the "Palm" mark from their domain names with exclusion from participation in Palm's marketing programs and with trademark infringement actions. A shorter letter explaining the problem and asking for input on a solution may have gotten a better response. Once Palm began the dialogue, it could have followed up with the detailed instructions on using the mark. Although Palm's letter concludes by asking the recipient to "[p]lease contact me directly if you have questions or specific issues you would like us to address," that sentence does not sound like an invitation to dialogue.

Generally speaking, people who become aware of the importance of trademark rules take them seriously and appreciate instruction on how to implement them. People who simply learn about the rules without understanding their underlying rationale find the rules so picky that they seldom take them seriously. When a fan of a company abuses the trademark, the first step to resolving the issue amicably is education. The second step is open discussion. Often, the discussion does not generate an acceptable alternative. When this occurs, the fan, at this point educated by the process, generally complies without hard feelings. It is worth these extra steps to maintain company relations with a company's biggest fans—this is, in fact, the essence of branding.

Heavy-handed enforcement letters can also alienate potential allies in enforcing company trademarks. For example, American Airlines received a letter from an attorney representing the North Face, a producer of athletic gear and apparel. The North Face apparently wanted American's assistance in preventing the importation of counterfeit goods bearing "The North Face" trademark. Instead of asking nicely, however, the attorney sent American the following:

> This firm represents The North Face, Inc. ("TNF"), a famous maker of high-performance climbing and backpacking equipment, mountaineering apparel, sportswear and accessories (the "TNF Products") since at least as early as 1968. As part of our representation of TNF, we are charged with the world-wide protection of TNF's brand identity.
>
> TNF is the owner of various trademarks throughout the world, including but not limited to THE NORTH FACE (U.S. Reg. No. 983,624; Canadian Ser. No. 1,095,797; Chinese Reg. Nos. 904,996, 917,789 and 909,919, and Chinese Ser. No. 96-0100487), THE NORTH FACE and Design (U.S. Reg. Nos. 2,097,715 and 2,300, 758 and Chinese Ser. No. 95-0100488) and MISCELLANEOUS DESIGN (U.S. Reg. Nos. 1,030,071 and 1,102,407; Canadian Ser. No. 1,095,796 and Chinese Reg. Nos. 917,788 and 909,920) (the "TNF Trademarks"). TNF has expended substantial efforts and funds to establish and market TNF Products, and as a result of these efforts and of the continuous and extensive use of the TNF Trademarks, those marks have acquired substantial goodwill and value as source identifiers for TNF and TNF Products.
>
> It has come to TNF's attention that certain of AMR

Corporation's, d/b/a American Airlines ("American"), employees may have returned in the past, and perhaps are still returning, from Asia (and in particular, China) with counterfeit TNF Products for their personal use and also, in many cases, for resale. To the extent American's employees may believe they have received a great bargain on TNF Products offered for sale at unusually low prices at retail markets like the Silk Market in Beijing or similar markets elsewhere in Asia, please be advised that there are *no* such bargains. Goods bearing famous trademarks for such low prices in these kinds of Asian markets are virtually always counterfeits, and more importantly, as genuine TNF Products are available only from retailers, distributors, and licensees authorized by TNF.

As we approach the Fall and Winter seasons, TNF anticipates a sharp increase in the incidence of such purchases by airline personnel who regularly travel between the United States and Asia, especially China. As you are aware, trafficking of counterfeit goods is highly illegal and those engaging in such activities, whether directly or indirectly, may be subject to civil and criminal liability under applicable United States and Canadian laws.

While we recognize that airline personnel may appear to be only a part of the counterfeiting problem, the regularity and frequency of their travel creates substantial traffic in counterfeit products. Moreover, in its aggregate, the continuing harm sustained by TNF, its valuable intellectual property, and its products as a direct result of American's employees' counterfeit trafficking is quite substantial.

We are writing both to advise you of TNF's intention to protect and enforce its valuable trademarks and goodwill vigorously and to enlist your assistance in addressing this problem. TNF will not tolerate any infringement of its intellectual property rights, and will investigate and prosecute each violator to the fullest extent permitted by law without further notice. Whether your company has an anti-counterfeiting policy in place already or adopts one as a result of this letter, we are specifically requesting that American take all necessary and appropriate steps to ensure that all personnel are on notice that such activities violate U.S. and Canadian laws and will not be tolerated by TNF (or, we hope, American). Such steps should include, at minimum, advising all employees throughout the company, in writing, of TNF's position.

We would greatly appreciate your confirmation that American has read this letter and implemented the steps urged therein. Needless to say, if you require any further information or have any questions, please do not hesitate to contact the undersigned.

Very Truly Yours,

This letter did not have the intended effect. It asked for American's assistance, but offered no means of helping to pay for it. It leveled vague and unsubstantiated allegations (American "employees *may have* returned in the past, and *perhaps* are still returning, from Asia (and in particular, China) with counterfeit TNF Products . . ."). And worst of all, the letter was poorly researched: American did not even fly to China. How much more effective would the letter have been if the attorney had simply written the following:

Re: THE NORTH FACE (U.S. Reg. No. 983,624; Canadian Ser. No. 1,095,797; Chinese Reg. Nos. 904,996, 917,789 and 909,919, and Chinese Ser. No. 96-0100487), THE NORTH FACE and Design (U.S. Reg. Nos. 2,097,715 and 2,300, 758 and Chinese Ser. No. 95-0100488) and MISCELLANEOUS DESIGN (U.S. Reg. Nos. 1,030,071 and 1,102,407; Canadian Ser. No. 1,095,796 and Chinese Reg. Nos. 917,788 and 909,920) (collectively "The North Face Trademarks").

The North Face, Inc. has become increasingly concerned about the importation from foreign countries of counterfeit goods bearing The North Face Trademarks. It has recently come to our attention that airline employees may be using their flight privileges to import such goods themselves or are providing flight benefits to those who do. While we do not at this time have specific evidence that any particular employee of American has participated in this activity, we worry that airline employees, due to their frequency of travel, may be tempted to purchase and import counterfeit goods bearing The North Face Trademarks. I am sure American does not condone the illegal importation of counterfeit goods or wish to see it continue.

The North Face believes that the people at American want to do the right thing. It also believes that most people want genuine THE NORTH FACE goods, not counterfeit goods of inferior quality. People who are properly educated will not participate in such activities or assist those who do.

The North Face would like to assist American in educating its employees against illegally trafficking in counterfeit goods. The North Face has prepared a pamphlet, which I have enclosed, that it would like to distribute to American's employees. Of course, The North Face will pay for the pamphlets and their distribution. In addition, if American does not have a policy prohibiting its employees from importing counterfeit goods, then this firm stands ready, at The North Face's expense, to help American create such a policy. Can The North Face get American's cooperation on this important issue? Thank you for your assistance and prompt response.

Sincerely,

Like the first letter, this revised letter puts American on notice of potential trademark infringement. The revised letter corrects several deficiencies, however. First, it does not make unsubstantiated allegations about company employees. Second, it proposes a direct course of action and provides the means to achieve it. Third, it does not attempt to threaten or bully a potential ally.

An initial contact with a potential infringer does not need to be threatening. In fact, many recipients of such letters will cooperate with the trademark owner if that option is available. Should the infringer fail to cooperate, the letters can escalate in tone and threatened consequences.

**Tips on trademark enforcement:**

1. As most categories of potential infringers may be misguided friends of the company, initial trademark-enforcement letters should not be overly threatening or demanding.

2. It is worth the time to tailor a trademark-enforcement letter to each specific situation rather than sending out form letters demanding compliance.

3. Because trademark-enforcement letters project the company's brand image, company lawyers should confer with marketing or corporate communications specialists as to the general form of enforcement letters.

4. If a polite letter does not receive an adequate response, later letters can escalate the tone and threatened consequences of continued noncompliance.

# Minding the ®s and ™s: Using the Appropriate Trademark Designations

You will often hear people confronted with trademark abuse respond with "Well, I put the ® there!" These people believe that the ® is some kind of cross that the trademark owner can hold out to ward off any evil that might befall the mark. This is the most dangerous myth regarding trademarks. Indiscriminately placing ®s next to company trademarks can lead to a monumental disaster.

While it is true that failing to place an ® next to a registered trademark can impair a trademark owner from recovering damages in an infringement action, this is not necessarily the case, particularly when the ® appears on other uses of the registered mark. By contrast, the consequences of misusing an ® can be severe. Courts have viewed this as a fraud on the public and have refused to enforce a trademark as a result. Thus, it is better to err on the side of caution in applying ®s to trademarks and to *not* apply them when one does not know whether the mark is or is not registered. Furthermore, it is extremely dangerous for someone who does not even know what the ® means to be applying it to trademarks.

Indiscriminate use of the ™ can also carry consequences. Because the ™ does not represent a claim regarding registration, it can be applied to registered and unregistered marks. However, indiscriminately applying the ™ to virtually every word in the corporate lexicon can indicate that the brand owner is attempting to reserve terms that are not trademarks. Courts take the use of these symbols seriously. It is surprising but true that a few misuses of two little symbols can cause so much trouble.

Federal registration in the United States does not mean that the mark is registered in any other country. Thus, advertising collateral directed at another country should use the trademark designation appropriate for that country and not the trademark designation for the United States. If collateral is directed at more than one country, then use the trademark designation appropriate to the country of printing (if the collateral is to be directed there) and include the notation "Printed in the country of printing, e.g. "U.S.A" on the collateral.

For international companies, it is important to retain registration information on all countries and make this information readily available to those who use the mark in those countries. Because marks are often used on short notice and tight deadlines, people should be able to check registration status on their own. An intranet or limited access Internet site is ideal for this purpose. Because registrations must be renewed, this information must be kept up to date. In addition, the brand standards manual and single trademark source should state that the ® symbol next to the mark (if pictured) is for the United States only and that collateral prepared for other countries needs to be checked for the appropriate trademark designation.

Companies should educate employees and other professionals on using the registration symbol with the brand, and adopt the following rules of use:

- Apply the ® symbol next to a registered trademark only. In all other instances, use the ™ or SM symbol.

- If you are unsure whether the mark is registered or not, apply the ™ or SM symbol. Do not ever apply the ® symbol next to a mark when you are unsure about registration.

- Registration status can change. Check for registration before applying an ® next to a mark.

**Tips on creating programs to ensure appropriate trademark designations are used:**

1. Educate employees on the consequences of applying an ® to an unregistered mark. Explode the myth that applying the registration symbol is sufficient to meet all legal requirements for using the mark.

2. Instruct employees not to use the ® except in circumstances where they know the mark is registered.

3. Set up a readily available source of information on registration

status, preferably a Web site that does not need to return phone calls to people working on a tight deadline.

# Playing It Again: Creating Brand Standards

Uniform branding is important both from a marketing and legal perspective. From a marketing perspective, a unified look promotes ready identification of the brand, strengthens the brand presence in consumer minds, and provides a sense of stability, consistency, and reliability. From a legal perspective, radical inconsistency in the brand can result in a finding that the brand does not constitute a trademark.

A brand-standards manual is the primary means for communicating brand standards to employees, licensees, and vendors. At a larger company, the brand-standards manual should originate from a committee with representatives from departments that frequently use the marks, such as marketing, legal, art, franchising, licensing, real estate, and communications.

The brand-standards manual's content will vary depending on the needs of the company, but most manuals should contain the following:

- statement of purpose of the manual;
- the brand's core values;
- samples of each trademark and specific applications for each, including:
  o color (including spot color and four color process)
  o reversed
  o trapped
  o backgrounds
  o size
  o typeface
  o grid scale
  o placement on labels
  o trademark designations (®, ™, SM, etc.);
- samples of acceptable and unacceptable uses for each trademark and trade name;
- use
  o print advertising

- o radio advertising
- o television advertising
- o packaging and labels
- o business cards, stationary, and envelopes
- o media communications
- o signs
- o vehicles;
- contacts;
- legal requirements
  - o rules of trademark use
  - o copyright notice and printing location
  - o truth in advertising rules
  - o required disclosures.

The brand-standards manual should succinctly state why each section is important, but should not reveal any attorney-client privileges or trade secrets, as it will be shared with advertisers, licensees, and others. All employees should have access to the brand-standards manual. At a minimum, employees should know the brand's core values and seek to incorporate them into their daily activities.

Companies should also conduct internal policing to ensure that the brand as used meets the requirements of the brand-standards manual. This function can be independently directed by a department that frequently uses the marks or be delegated to the auditing department as part of regular audits.

Enforcing brand standards is not an enjoyable task. Many employees see brand standards as a form of oppression that squashes their creativity. Getting corporate managers to buy into brand standards and the mantra "be creative except with the trademark" makes brand standards much easier to enforce. Usually, a conversation with front-line managers about the value of the trademark and how easily it can be lost will convince them to help with enforcement.

Finally, making the brand-standards manual the single source for obtaining camera-ready copies of the company trademarks at least forces those who want to use the trademarks to see the brand-standards manual as well. Creating a click agreement pop-up that states "I will use this trademark in accordance with the brand-standards manual" before allowing the user to download the trademark will reinforce the manual's importance and ease the enforcement burden.

**Tips on creating brand standards:**

1. Brand consistency reinforces the brand in consumer minds and helps prevent brand abandonment.
2. Creating a brand-standards manual will help maintain brand consistency and prevent legal problems regarding the trademark.
3. All employees should have access to the brand-standards manual. Employees should learn the brand's core values and how the brand represents those values.
4. Conduct internal policing to ensure brand consistency. Getting front-line managers to buy in on brand standards will reduce the enforcement burden.
5. Make the brand-standards manual the single source for obtaining camera-ready copies of the trademark.

# The Benefits and Risks of Licensing

Brand licensing has numerous benefits, but also some major risks. Probably the best way to avoid the risks is to make sure the licensing program is professionally developed and managed, either by an in-house professional with licensing experience or a trademark-management firm. Many trademark-management firms operate on commission, allowing the brand owner to profit without a major financial investment. A trademark-management firm can generate new licensees, introduce co-branding opportunities, monitor existing licensees, and send trademark-enforcement letters to place infringers under license. The brand owner should monitor the trademark-management firm to make sure it is performing up to standards.

Licensing can provide the following benefits to a brand owner:

- Increasing the legal protection afforded the mark. Trademarks are generally registered in the categories in which the mark is used. By increasing the classifications of products under the mark, licensing provides trademarks with a broader scope of legal protection. For example, ABC Delivery Company's mark falls under class 39 (transportation and storage) because ABC uses the mark in picking up, storing, transporting, and delivering documents, packages, and freight by land and air. By creating toy vehicles bearing the "ABC Delivery" mark, ABC expands its protection to class 28 (toys and sporting goods). Because ABC is not in the toy business, a licensing program offers ABC an efficient entry into this market.

- Resolving infringement actions. Licensing offers a compromise position to the all-or-nothing infringement action. Trademark cases are high stakes, winner-take-all litigation with little room to compromise. Consents to use often wind up being used against the consenting mark owner. A licensing program allows the mark owner to offer a compromise position, and earn revenue as well. Harley-Davidson has one of the world's most beloved marks— people tattoo it permanently on their bodies. Unfortunately, the company allowed so much infringement on the mark that the mark was almost abandoned. Finding the most unsympathetic infringer it could—a pornographer—Harley Davidson sued for trademark infringement and pulled out a narrow victory. Armed with the opinion, Harley-Davidson's legal counsel began sending out trademark infringement letters and signed up many infringers as licensees. The legal department actually began generating revenue, needed by the company that was in dire financial straights. Harley-Davidson, of course, recovered financially, has a strong and profitable licensing program, and has a brand that the 2002 Interbrand survey values at $6.27 billion.

- Expanding brand recognition and exposure. Placing a brand on other products, even those unrelated to the core business, can give a sense of brand pervasiveness, providing significant advertising support. Note the success of Caterpillar's licensing program, which seems to have placed a CAT logo hat on every other head in the Midwest. Caterpillar has leveraged this program to help create a corporate image of strength and durability. The program has also helped glamorize Caterpillar's core business, which is amazing considering it basically consists of making machines that dig holes in the ground. In fact, Interbrand cited Caterpillar's licensing program in valuing the "Caterpillar" brand at $3.22 billion, observing that Caterpillar had "steamrolled into merchandise and clothing, playing off its rough-and-tumble image." Similarly, many states prohibit the sale of whisky, the core product of Jack Daniel's, in grocery stores. By marketing "Jack Daniel's" charcoal (which is used in filtering "Jack Daniel's" whisky), the company placed its brand in grocery stores and found a way to sell what was previously a waste product from its manufacturing process. Interbrand valued the "Jack Daniel's" brand at $1.58 billion in 2002.

- Increased revenue. Licensing offers opportunities to diversify the business, obtain royalty income streams without a significant monetary investment, and capitalize on unrealized brand equity.

Licensing can even generate flow-back revenue by creating "fans" of the product that would not otherwise exist. For example, how many children become fans of sports teams after receiving a T-shirt or hat bearing the team logo? The same principle works with soft drinks, food, lodging, and other goods and services. Sometimes, these loyalties forged in youth (or even adulthood) result in a lifetime of purchases for the licensor's core product.

- Entry into new product markets. Licensing can provide entry into markets where the company either lacks brand recognition or expertise. For example, BASF Wyandotte wanted to launch a national brand for its antifreeze, but shuddered at the estimated $15-million annual cost of developing national brand recognition and distribution. On the other hand, the STP Products Co. desired to market antifreeze but lacked the expertise and production capacity. STP and BASF solved their problems with a license agreement marketing BASF manufactured antifreeze under the "STP" brand.

- Entry into unfamiliar geographic markets. Licensing can also provide entry into geographic markets where the company lacks sufficient knowledge of local customs and consumer desires. Everyone knows the story about the Coca-Cola Company running a translated advertisement in China that promised to bring ancestors back from the dead. By licensing the brand to a manufacturer or distributor with a solid local reputation and knowledge of the local market, the company can minimize the risk of expanding into new geographic areas, as well as minimize shipping costs. In the 1980s, the "Lowenbrau" brand rapidly boosted international sales and brand recognition through worldwide licensing agreements without the expense of creating overseas bottling plants.

Licensing, however, is not without risks:

- Naked licenses. Ironically, a company trying to trade off its brand equity has to put the brand at risk to do so. Adequate monitoring

125

can prevent a naked license, but the company must apply resources to a monitoring program. Companies unwilling to make a commitment to monitoring products produced under license should not engage in a licensing program.

- Product overexposure. Riding the 1980s resurgence in prep culture, General Mills went on a tear licensing the "IZOD" mark to manufacturers who were not Ivy League. Some of the manufacturers went Borneo (in preppy parlance), so General Mills had to engage in some heavy legal action. Because the "IZOD" mark appeared on everything from wallets to key chains to sunglasses, preps jacked out to see the mark on people who were definitely Not Our Kind, Dear and began bolting the reptile for the polo player. General Mills' profits from the "IZOD" mark fell 25 percent in fiscal 1984.

- Shoddy products. Nothing destroys brand equity faster than negative consumer experiences. If a brewery licenses its name to a maker of rancid wine, what will people think about its beer? Even unrelated products can affect consumer views. If an airline licenses its marks to a manufacturer who makes toy airplanes that fall apart, what will people think of the company's real planes? In an industry where safety is a paramount concern, shoddy products are unacceptable.

- Business disputes. Licensees do not always get along with their licensors. Disputes can arise over product quality, access to the licensor's internal markets, licensor inaction against infringement, cannibalization of the licensee's market, and inadequate support by the licensor for the licensed brand. Making sure the licensor and licensee share the same goals is essential to avoiding later disputes.

Understanding the rewards and risks of licensing can lead to effective licensing programs. To create an effective licensing program:

- Create a strategy. The strategy should reflect the brand's core values and the overall corporate strategy. General Mills' licensing program for the "IZOD" brand ran contrary to the product's core value: exclusivity. Caterpillar's licensing program reflects its core values: strength and durability.

- Coordinate among licensees. In the 1980s, the Weight Watchers organization started a licensing program for food carrying the "Weight Watchers" mark. However, Weight Watchers did not coordinate the initial name and logo presentation among the licensees, which lessened the initial impact of the program.

- Provide access to internal markets. Assist the licensee by providing access to captive audiences, such as employees and customers, so long as this access will not interfere with the core business. For example, most airlines offer their licensed products in their in-flight catalogues, providing licensees with a captive market of potential customers. Providing licensees opportunities to create special products for employees, such as company logo apparel, allows both the licensee and the company to take advantage of economies of scale and thus reduces costs.

- Monitor and coach. Offering licensees genuine assistance with their efforts makes monitoring more palatable and less oppressive, and also adds value to both parties' mutual benefit. Questor Corporation, which owned the "Spaulding" brand, lost $12 million making all its own products in 1980. By 1983, Questor licensees made all "Spaulding" products, and Questor made a $12 million profit. Questor did not make its licensees work alone. It sent marketing executives with its licensees' salespeople into the field and maintained a large staff of sporting-goods designers to maintain product leadership.

- Be up front. Licensors should explain the marketing plan for the brand after obtaining a nondisclosure agreement from the licensee. This will allow the licensee to understand its role in the process, suggest new marketing opportunities to the licensor, and enter the arrangement with accurate expectations. The licensee also needs to understand the brand's core values and how the product under license supports the company's overall strategic plan. A licensee that cannot be trusted with this information cannot be trusted with the brand. Of course, where a trademark license evolves out of infringement litigation, licensors should exercise caution in disclosing information to the licensee.

**Tips on creating an effective licensing program:**

1.  Understand the risks of licensing and address them up front with a potential licensee. Allow the licensee to understand the brand core values, brand standards, and marketing plan.

2.  Implement a coordinated licensing strategy that supports the brand's core values. Be able to articulate why a particular license supports the core values.

3.  Add value to the license beyond the brand itself. Assist the licensee by providing access to the company's internal markets and promotional activities.

# SUMMARY

This book presents a history of colossal branding failures. Failures that permanently wiped out brands of incredible value. Failures that could have been avoided, and yet were repeated time and again over the past 100 years. Yet in the hundreds of cases reporting these failures, each failure generally comes down to one of three different scenarios: the mark owner either abandoned the brand, caused the brand to become generic, or defrauded the public. It really is that simple.

Marks were abandoned either through non-use, excessive modification, failure to police infringement, or failure to properly license the mark and/or monitor the licensee. Marks were ruled generic because the brand owner started out with an indefensible brand, failed to take action against public misuse of the brand, or used the brand in a manner that encouraged public misuse by defining it, failing to use it as a proper adjective, or failing to distinguish it in text. Courts found brand owners defrauded the public by falsely claiming registration status or by adopting a deceptive mark.

Many of these cases involved the world's largest and most sophisticated corporations. How is it that some of the world's largest corporations can, time and again, fail to learn from history and thus be doomed to repeat it? My only conclusion is that this has happened through ignorance. An editorial in the April 2003 edition of

*Information Today* represents this point of view by rhapsodizing:

> Ah, the painful agony of becoming so successful and important to the culture that your name crosses over into popular usage. In these cases, the runaway success of a product becomes its ultimate failure as a distinctive brand name. What a (marvelous) dilemma. [...] I may be stepping out of line here because I really haven't asked our lawyers, but I for one would be delighted if people respected this publication so much that they'd refer to the act of finding out what was happening in our industry as "InfoToday-ing."

This point of view is pervasive throughout advertising. What could be better than having your brand become synonymous with the product? Why wouldn't you want to encourage everyone to put your brand everywhere they can?

Obviously, the proponents of this point of view fail to see the brand as property. But like it or not, the brand is property, and must be treated as such or it will be lost. If you don't believe your brand is valuable property, you are probably right, because that belief has permeated your organization and made it virtually impossible to build a valuable brand.

The keys to creating, maintaining, and protecting a valuable brand are:

- Recognizing the necessity of brand exclusivity, and that a brand that anyone can use lacks value;
- Understanding the brand's value to the business;
- Knowing what the brand represents and clearly articulating a brand message and strategy throughout the organization;
- Learning the rules of brand use.

People who learn the rules of brand use and understand their underlying rationale know how to preserve the brand's value. In fact, they become forever changed in that they can never look at advertising the same way. They notice when an advertisement breaks the brand use rules. They wonder why companies with brands worth millions and even billions of dollars would put those brands at risk with slogans like:

Don't worry. There's a FedEx for that.

Stop Cleaning. Start Swiffering.

Do you Yahoo?

Do these slogans guarantee that those brands will be destroyed? Obviously not. It is difficult to determine how a court will decide a given case, particularly based on a single fact. But it is also true that courts have cited slogans like those above in declaring a brand generic. Following the trademark use rules, instead of ignoring them, offers the best hope for protecting a brand.

# APPENDIX
## *Brand Use Rules*

The following is a short guide to the rules of use. More detailed descriptions of each rule can be found beginning on the cited pages.

### General Rules of Use

1. Use it or lose it. Page 27.
*Rule:* A trademark can be canceled for non-use.

2. Don't contribute the mark to the English language. Page 29.
*Rule:* Keep the mark out of the dictionary and the public domain.

3. Don't give the mark a split personality. Page 32.
*Rule:* Do not give the mark a definition. Use the mark as a trademark alone, not as the name of the product.

4. Put it in writing. Page 34.
*Rule:* Don't grant others permission to use the mark without a written contract.

5. Watch 'em like a hawk. Page 37.
*Rule:* Monitor those who use the mark under contract.

6. Keep their grubby hands off the mark. Page 41.
*Rule:* Prevent others from infringing on the mark.

7. Mind the ®s and ™s. Page 43.

*Rule:* Use the appropriate trademark designation. Trademark owners may not claim that an unregistered mark is registered.

*Rule:* The ® is symbolic of a trademark registered with the appropriate governmental authorities. ™ and $^{SM}$ mean that the owner is claiming trademark status, but is not making any claim about registration.

*Rule:* Stating that a mark "is a registered trademark of" an entity is a claim that the trademark is registered with the appropriate governmental authorities. Stating that a mark "is a trademark of" an entity is a claim to trademark status without a claim of registration.

8. Play it again, Sam. Page 45.

*Rule:* Use a mark in a consistent manner.

## Rules for Using Trademarks in Text

1. Don't let the mark stand alone. Page 48.

*Rule:* When using the mark in a sentence, always use the mark as an adjective to modify a noun. Never use the mark as a noun or a verb.

2. Make the mark stand out in the crowd. Page 50.

*Rule:* Distinguish the mark from the remaining text. Use some method of alerting the reader that they are seeing a mark instead of an ordinary word.

3. Don't give the mark an identity crisis. Page 53.

*Rule:* When the mark is similar to the company name (e.g., "Acme, Inc." uses the mark "ACME"), do not use the mark to refer to the company name. Similarly, do not use the company name as the mark.

4. Don't let the mark lose its way home. Page 57.

*Rule:* When using a company domain name or address as a mark, do not use the mark as a domain name or address. Do not make directional information appear like a mark, and do not make the mark appear like directional information.

# LIST OF AUTHORITIES

# LIST OF AUTHORITIES

# ACKNOWLEDGMENTS

I would first like to thank the great folks at Barricade Books for making this book's publication a reality, in particular Lyle Stuart and Carole Stuart for believing in me and giving me a shot, Jeff Nordstedt for being my mentor throughout the publication process, my hard-working editor Sandy Stuart, and Jennifer Itskevich for her great publicity ideas and efforts. Second, I would like to thank Akin Gump Strauss Hauer & Feld LLP for being a great place to work that supports the development of its attorneys, and in particular I'd like to thank John M. Cone, Orrin L. Harrison, III, Katherine Kurtz, Daniel J. Micciche, and Gevona Plaster. Third, I would like to thank the people that read this book, provided valuable feedback, and ultimately gave their endorsements of the book. You are some of the most impressive people I know. I asked you to review the book because I have the greatest respect for your opinions. It pleased me to no end that you liked it. Fourth, I would like to thank my personal attorneys, Andrew Yung and John Scott of Scott Yung LLP in Dallas, Texas. There are no two finer lawyers in the world. Fifth, I have been blessed throughout my career to have mentors who took the time to pass on to me their skills and knowledge, and supported me when I needed them most. Specifically: Anne and Robert Banse, Barry C. Barnett, Randall P. Bezanson, Herbert L. Costner, T. Thomas Cottingham, III, Kay Frapart, Karen B. Fredenburg, Thomas R. Goodwin, Avery (Pete) Guest, Frank A. Hirsch, Jr., Paul F. Kirgis, R. Laurence Macon, Ruth McRea, George A. (Trey) Nicoud III, Jodi O'Brien, Terrell W. Oxford, Phyllis J. Sawyers, Andrew D. Shore, and Stephen D. Susman. Sixth, I would like to thank my family for their constant support: Margaret, Bob, Ellene, Tom, Andy, Tim, Jerry, Yvette, Ashley, Blake, and Brooke. Finally and most importantly, I'd like to thank my wife Jennifer for supporting me and this project, and for being the very best. This never would have been possible without you.

# INDEX

# INDEX

# INDEX